D1756456

Public Art

3 0 JUL 2025

WITHDRAWN

York St John University

3 8025 00603307 3

For Beatrix Marcel –

I love you the whole world.

3 0 JUL 2023

Public Art:
Theory, Practice and Populism

Cher Krause Knight

YORK ST. JOHN
LIBRARY & INFORMATION
SERVICES

Blackwell
Publishing

© 2008 Cher Krause Knight

BLACKWELL PUBLISHING
350 Main Street, Malden, MA 02148-5020, USA
9600 Garsington Road, Oxford OX4 2DQ, UK
550 Swanston Street, Carlton, Victoria 3053, Australia

The right of Cher Krause Knight to be identified as the author of this work has been asserted in accordance with the UK Copyright, Designs, and Patents Act 1988.

All rights reserved. No part of this publication may be reproduced, stored in a retrieval system, or transmitted, in any form or by any means, electronic, mechanical, photocopying, recording or otherwise, except as permitted by the UK Copyright, Designs, and Patents Act 1988, without the prior permission of the publisher.

Designations used by companies to distinguish their products are often claimed as trademarks. All brand names and product names used in this book are trade names, service marks, trademarks, or registered trademarks of their respective owners. The publisher is not associated with any product or vendor mentioned in this book.

This publication is designed to provide accurate and authoritative information in regard to the subject matter covered. It is sold on the understanding that the publisher is not engaged in rendering professional services. If professional advice or other expert assistance is required, the services of a competent professional should be sought.

First published 2008 by Blackwell Publishing Ltd

4   2012

Library of Congress Cataloging-in-Publication Data is available for this book

ISBN 978-1-4051-5558-8 (hardback)
ISBN 978-1-4051-5559-5 (paperback)

A catalogue record for this title is available from the British Library.

Set in 11/13.5pt Galliard
by SPi Publisher Services, Pondicherry, India
Printed and bound in Singapore
by Markono Print Media Pte Ltd

The publisher's policy is to use permanent paper from mills that operate a sustainable forestry policy, and which has been manufactured from pulp processed using acid-free and elementary chlorine-free practices. Furthermore, the publisher ensures that the text paper and cover board used have met acceptable environmental accreditation standards.

For further information on
Blackwell Publishing, visit our website at
www.blackwellpublishing.com

Contents

Contents

Preface

The role of the spectator is to determine the weight of the work on the esthetic scale. (Duchamp 1957: 819)

I cannot think of a single book on public art that commences with Marcel Duchamp. Maybe this is not surprising. Duchamp, the irreverent artist-provocateur, is best known as a Dadaist. Confounded by the massive violence of World War I, the Dada artists responded to senseless cruelty and destruction with artworks that trafficked in absurdity, mocking conventional art world pretensions. Dadaism was a social movement as much as an artistic one; the aforementioned "esthetic scale" actually encompassed much more than aesthetics. Audiences were asked to interrogate the foundations of society, moving beyond collective and individual comfort zones. Dadaism represented an unwillingness to accept things as they are, resisting complicit endorsement of the status quo. "Spectators" bore a great responsibility – if not to change their behaviors, at least to question the social norms that formed them. Duchamp instinctively apprehended the viewer's primary role in the art experience. In "The Creative Act" (1957), he scrutinizes the authority of the artist, and affirms the power of the spectator. He describes the "art coefficient" as a gap between an artist's intention and the artwork's realization, where viewers actively engage with and interpret the art. Duchamp proposes that an artist cannot fully express his own intent, so the viewer must complete the Creative Act;

without someone to react to and interact with the art, the artistic process is forever unfinished, a still-born idea never seizing its absolute potential. No longer a passive act, "viewing" gives way to a multitude of readings, limited only by the number of people in a work's audience. Duchamp offered a potent analogy, describing art in its "raw state" as molasses, which is then "refined" into pure sugar by its spectators (1957: 818–19). The artist provides the source material, but it is the viewer – with her own viewpoint, taste, education, and experience – who discerns its meaning and relevance. Once art is shared with a larger public, the artist surrenders control to the unpredictable will and whims of "the people."

In the glossary of *New-Land-Marks* public art is defined as "art placed in public places and spaces," and those spaces as "open to everyone to use and enjoy" (Bach 2001: 153). If only it were that easy! The contours of art's publicness are continually assessed on its physical location. But as Hilde Hein asserts, "The sheer presence of art out-of-doors or in a bus terminal or a hotel reception area does not automatically make that art public – no more than placing a tiger in a barnyard would make it a domestic animal" (1996: 4). I suggest we can best understand art's public functions when we consider the interrelationship between content and audience; what art has to say, to whom it speaks, and the multiple messages it may convey. This approach prompts several questions: Is public art's responsibility "to communicate with the public"? To do so, must it transcend an artist's private or aesthetic concerns, and "generate human reaction" from a larger audience (Doezema 1977: 9, 14)? If so, how big must that audience be? As early as 1903 Charles Mulford Robinson's *Modern Civic Art* called for art that was comprehensible and socially relevant to its audiences, addressing "the conditions before their very eyes" (1903: 34). But the notion of a shared artistic vocabulary has long since dissipated; as Arlene Raven contends, "public art isn't a hero on a horse any more" (1989: 1). Through his experiences as a public art administrator Jerry Allen observed that the civic symbolism of the past was a language in which the public was no longer "fluent." He queries: "Can substantially fewer than everybody be the audience for public art without destroying the public character of the art?" Allen concludes that since public art is "broad and heterogeneous," speaking to wide though not necessarily large and generalized audiences, it would be best to define a "new public" for each work (1985: 246–7, 250–1). For Patricia Phillips art only becomes fully public when it takes "the idea of public as the genesis and subject for analysis": "it is public because of the kinds of questions it chooses to ask or address, and not because of its accessibility or volume of viewers" (1992: 298). To this I would add that art's publicness rests in the quality and impact of its exchanges with audiences. These do not hinge on wide acceptance, but on the art's ability to extend reasonable and fair opportunities for members of the public to understand and negotiate their own relationships with it. I propose to conceive public art primarily through this populist agenda.

A few words must be said about the frictions – perceived and actual – between art elitists and populists, although caution must be exercised when dealing in such binaries. Generally, elitists emphasize the need for professionalism and formal education in the arts, art-specific institutions, and standards of quality according to established canons of taste. For them the boundaries of culture are fixed though fragile; they are perceived as centurions standing guard over and imposing their culture on others. Conversely, populists usually argue for the widest possible availability of art experiences, welcome cultural diversity, and promote public (often "amateur") participation in and experiential relationships to art. Their pluralistic construction of artistic merit, open-ended definitions of taste, and insistence on art's subjectivity and mutability prompt elitists to charge them with eroding culture's quality and substance. These conflicting agendas result in what Margaret Wyszomirski identified as "the tension between the quest for excellence and the quest of equality." She concludes that these "quests" might coalesce in a framework of cultural democracy, if we temper the notion of "elite" art audiences with "open-door exclusivity" (1982: 13–14, 17; Levine 1988: 255). I interpret this as an egalitarian impulse; to provide all interested parties with an entrée into the arts that nurtures confidence in their own critical faculties, but allows final decisions about engagement to rest with each individual. Yet such agency can be hampered by what Miwon Kwon identifies as art's great myth: the presumption that it is "good" and "everybody wants it" (Arning, Chin, Jacob, and Kwon 2006).

Edward Arian outlined the premises of cultural democracy: art experiences develop good citizenship and enhance the quality of life; all citizens have the right to art experiences, the provision of which "is a public responsibility not unlike health and education"; and people of all backgrounds and classes are desirous of art experiences when presented with options to engage in such. These principles manifest themselves in a specifically populist approach as codified in American arts legislation: emphasis on broad-based exposure to and consumption of the arts; conviction that art contributes to individual humanistic growth; a belief that government should foster each citizen's development on behalf of its own welfare; the need to showcase and support the talent of artists; and an effort to make the arts part of people's everyday lives. But Arian asserts that cultural democracy exists only when people are able to assess "their cultural needs and determine the programs that will best meet those needs and express their individual identities" (1989: 3–5, 24–9; Kardon 1980: 8). Though disparate, the sites and works of decidedly populist public art share at least one if not all of the following three qualities. First, they create immersive, experiential environments: instead of building independent objects around which audiences must negotiate, designers usually produce enveloping settings to traverse through. Next, each engenders highly proactive relationships with visitors, predicated on participatory interaction, not passive viewership. And finally, they are frequently private ventures or public–private partnerships; without portending to a false sense of egalitarianism, these are often more inviting and potentially civic-spirited than their typical public art counterparts.

In 1981 John Beardsley argued that most discussions of public art were limited to issues of physical rather than emotional or intellectual accessibility (1981b: 43). Since that time there have been many efforts to broaden public art's accessibility, with mixed results. I contend that art becomes most fully public when it has palpable populist sentiments – *the extension of emotional and intellectual, as well as physical, accessibility to the audience* – not a pretension toward such. Unfettered physical access is an empty gesture if the public does not feel other forms of accessibility are within its grasp too. Accordingly the placement, funding, and content of public art will be scrutinized here as related to audience engagement. Assessments of audience response made throughout the text are based upon years of research, including my personal observations of and conversations with members of the public. The book begins with an overview of American public art's "official" history since the early twentieth century, when governmental programs nurtured notions of cultural democracy. The second chapter considers artworks that fit within conventional paradigms of public art, but evidence heightened populist intent. Chapter 3 examines interrelationships between art museums and public art, and queries how museums can further enhance their well-intentioned attempts at civic engagement. In the fourth chapter we encounter private patrons and industry that have succeeded in capturing the public's imagination, and ask what public artists and administrators can learn from them. Chapter 5 argues for viewers' increased agency to determine the levels of engagement with art and merits of their own art experiences, whether these be intentional or not. The concluding chapter addresses some persistent woes that often accompany public art and works that manage to avoid these, highlighting venues and situations in which populist public art thrives, and could do so in the future.

Although focused on the United States, the wider critical scope of the questions raised here is relevant to public art elsewhere. The US is a vast and greatly differentiated country, with nearly limitless local artistic dialects and regional cultures. In an increasingly pluralistic society, Beardsley reminds us, there are no coherent belief systems or definitive interpretations; "public values are not universal, but a function of their epoch and locale. ... An art that expresses the values of all the people is impossible to achieve" (1981b: 43–4). In *The Public and Its Problems*, John Dewey made much the same observation, noting that the "public" always changes with time and place, and suggesting that such a public is "too diffused and scattered and too intricate in composition" to be treated as a holistic entity (1927: 33, 137). An attempt to discern a unitary national aesthetic or any such consensus is futile. But while a single *vox populi* cannot exist, this book strives to identify and contextualize dominant or recurrent traits shared among the spectrum of American sensibilities, and provide a fuller understanding of our shared culture and more accurate barometers of our tastes. To do so will lead to some sources that critics might regard as unsophisticated or unworthy as "art." In his sensitive study of Holocaust memorials, James Young observes that traditional modes of art historical inquiry cannot fully accommodate the "social life" of public art, which fuses art, popular culture, historical memory, and political consequences. He proclaims: "Rather than patronizing mass tastes, we must recognize that public taste carries weight" (1993: 11–13). But while definitions of "high" and "low" culture continually shift, "popular culture" remains maligned by those seeking to "maintain their ideological authority by defining 'good' and 'bad' culture." We need to recognize popular culture as "a potentially powerful and progressive political force," which liberates its makers and users from "the top-down strictures of high culture" to subvert the "dominant notions of taste" (Jenkins, McPherson, and Shattuc 2002: 26–8).

In *No Respect: Intellectuals and Popular Culture*, Andrew Ross warns against taking a "conspiratorial view" of mass culture as a monolithic, "profitable opiate" imposed on a passive public of consumers that uncritically accepts such culture. He posits that critics who take such dim views of popular culture engage in an undemocratic sort of intellectual hysteria, or sample that culture only to reinforce their status as they are "slumming" it. Conversely, other critics unquestioningly embrace popular culture's "gee-whizzery" (1989: 4–5, 7, 45, 50–2). I wish to do none of the above. My populist perspective seeks balance between the hypercritical and uncritical nodes; to reorient our appreciation for artworks already absorbed into the canon, highlight the viewer's role, and suggest an expanded terrain for public art. The intent is not to measure "successes" and "failures," but rather to assess art's publicness and engage in a jargon-free discussion of its pertinent issues. By proposing a more widely constituted domain for the study and practice of public art, disparate artworks, organizations, and individuals might be able to coexist, if not agree. The complications brought by public art's complexity are also its opportunities. Though "public art" cannot be pinned down with a single, reductive definition, hopefully a more panoramic view of the field shall emerge here. Like Duchamp,

I recognize there is always a gap between intention and realization; this text strives to be informative and provocative, while leaving readers enough intellectual elbow room to reach different and contradictory conclusions. The book is in a perpetually "raw state," and readers are invited to visit their own "refinements" upon it.

Acknowledgments

Supposedly writing is a solitary journey, but without the help and support of others I could not have written this book. First I want to thank my editor, Jayne Fargnoli. She believed in this project from our first tentative conversation about it, and brought a keen intellect, kindness, and expert stewardship to every step of the process. Ken Provencher, Margot Morse, and Annette Abel were also invaluable resources, as have been the many other helpful people at Blackwell Publishing.

My colleagues at Emerson College, especially those in the Department of Visual and Media Arts (VMA), have been wonderfully encouraging and enthusiastic about the book. I would also like to thank the administration of Emerson College, particularly Jacqueline Liebergott, Linda Moore, Grafton Nunes, and Michael Selig. The College provided both financial and intellectual resources, most notably two Faculty Advancement Fund Grants that gave me precious time to work on the text, and the Mann Stearns Distinguished Faculty Award, which funded essential research travel. I must also acknowledge our excellent staff in the VMA department, including several terrific graduate assistants.

My students at Emerson have been a continued source of delight and enlightenment. In particular, those students in my public art seminar courses in the Fall 2005 and Fall 2006 semesters contributed greatly to my thoughts on this subject. Without all of you, this would have been a far different, and much less interesting, book.

Acknowledgments

I had many illuminating discussions along the way with colleagues, friends, and family that had direct bearing on the text, too many to mention though my thanks are sincere. Harriet Senie's intelligence, candor, and compassion made for an excellent sounding board on many occasions. She continues to remind me of the excitement to be found in public art. Mags Harries, Lajos Héder, and Robert Sabal all generously shared their time, art, and good conversation. Sam Binkley and Eric Gordon, who were writing their own books at the same time, offered empathic camaraderie. Therese Dolan, Gerald Silk, and Laura Watts Sommer manage to humanize academia when I need it most. And Brooke A. Knight, always my first and last reader, was a constant companion throughout the process. Not only did he offer moral support and constructive criticism, but he took several of the wonderful photographs included here.

I would also like to thank my parents, Harold and Elaine Krause, who accompanied me to see *The Gates* and reconfirmed my suspicion that public art had a different story to tell. And my daughter, Beatrix Marcel, who looks with her heart as much as her eyes.

Chapter 1   Introduction: A Short History of the United States' "Official" Public Art

Just six months before his tragic assassination in November 1963, John F. Kennedy responded to a report on the status of arts in the federal government he requested the year before. Writing to the report's author, August Heckscher, the President noted:

> Government can never take over the role of patronage and support filled by private individuals and groups in our society. But government surely has a significant part to play in helping establish the conditions under which art can flourish – in encouraging the arts as it encourages science and learning. (JFK qtd. in Netzer 1978: 58)

Here Kennedy staked an ideological claim for public support of the arts, building a foundation for the United States' official art patronage. Yet there remains no definitive interpretation of "exactly what public art is, or ought to be" (Allen 1985: 246). If we define "public art" by its most basic precepts, then its roots reach far back in history. Its works are conceived for larger audiences, and placed to garner their attention; meant to provide an edifying, commemorative, or entertaining experience; and convey messages through generally comprehensible content. Meeting the public on its daily travels, these artworks reinforced the agendas of those under whose aegis they were constructed: ranging from countless portraits of ancient rulers, designed to bolster confidence and inspire loyalty; to massive pieces of street furniture, like triumphal arches proclaiming

1

the military prowess of particular regimes. But the notion of art in the service of the people, rather than ruling factions, is a more modern concept. One thinks, for example, of citizens emboldened by the French Revolution demanding that the Louvre, a private palace housing royal treasures, be opened to the people of the Republic (which did happen on August 10, 1793). As Carol Duncan suggests, public art institutions and initiatives became "evidence of political virtue, indicative of a government that provided the right things for its people," while being "a preserver of past achievements and a provider for the common good" (1991: 88–9, 93, 101–2).

While many European nations have well-established, widely supported traditions of state patronage, it is only in the last century that the US made sustained efforts in this endeavor. Although the evolution of our government's arts patronage was not necessarily "orderly" (Prokopoff 1981: 78), it is illuminating. Americans remain admiring of European culture and even state support of it, though historically our attitudes toward the arts are "ambiguous and contradictory." In the absence of a "clear public philosophy regarding the value and place of art in society" (Wyszomirski 1982: 11), some citizens took it upon themselves to commission or make art. In 1872 Philadelphia neighbors Henry Fox and Charles Howell spearheaded the Fairmount Park Art Association, the US's first private nonprofit organization focused on integrating public art and urban planning. Still thriving today, the Association cooperates with civic agencies to commission artworks responsive to the city's layout and spirit (Bach 1988: 262–3). With the turn of the twentieth century came the short-lived but influential City Beautiful Movement, whose proponents, envious of European urbanism, contended that social responsibility and order would follow in the wake of meticulous planning. Charles Mulford Robinson epitomizes this mindset: he conceived of a "civic art" with utilitarian, moral, and educational functions, which "exists not for its own sake, but mainly for the good of the community" (1903: 26–9, 35). The Depression next advanced our government's arts patronage, but it was not until the 1960s that this role was formalized on more permanent terms. Garry Apgar posits that American pragmatism tends to resist state patronage for the arts, though he recognizes that "fundamentally democratic approaches to government support" have taken root here (1992: 24, 26). In this chapter we shall encounter three federal programs critical to the foundation and development of an "official" American public art: the New Deal art initiatives, which represented our first concerted effort to support artists while producing art underscoring state ideology; the General Services Administration's Art-in-Architecture program, in which a percentage of federal construction costs is allocated for the arts; and the no longer extant Art-in-Public-Places program of the National Endowment for the Arts, which offered matching grants to local communities. As we shall see, there are significant distinctions between cultural democracy "as a social idea" and political democracy "as a system of government" (Dewey 1927: 143).

Roosevelt's New Deal

The profound despair of life for many Americans in the 1930s (marked by the economic woes of the Great Depression and the Dust Bowl agricultural crisis) was offset by a series of socially pro-gressive programs. Combined under the umbrella of "The New Deal," these were conceived and managed by President Franklin Delano Roosevelt's administration. As Richard McKinzie asserts, the New Deal's intentions were altruistic: to attend to people's cere-bral needs as much as their material ones (1973). In addition to addressing unemployment, business failures, and a lack of adequate food and shelter, the New Deal also positioned the federal govern-ment as a primary agent of social change and enlightenment, entrusted to ensure the welfare of all citizens. Despite its shortcom-ings, the New Deal got many Americans "back to work," including artists employed in "the largest art program ever undertaken by the federal government" (Park and Markowitz 1992: 131). From 1933 to 1943 thousands of artists produced over a hundred thousand artworks under the patronage of the American government, though as Dick Netzer reminds us, this was a temporary measure. The impetus was less "a special concern for artistic activity … (or) a com-mitment to a permanent federal role in support of the arts," and more a matter of alleviating the dire economic climate (1978: 54).

First came the Public Works of Art Project (PWAP) in 1933, directed by Edward Bruce, which paid professional artists daily wages to make works for public buildings. But after seven short months it became clear that the PWAP's stopgap approach could not meet enduring needs. By 1935 the Federal Art Project (FAP), run under the Works Progress Administration (WPA), was established. The FAP remained intact until the New Deal's end in 1943, when the US's involvement in World War II intensified, and critics complained that any state-supported art smacked of fascism (Harris 1995: 153). The FAP, which was the largest and best-known of the art programs, served artists already on relief and disseminated their artworks to state and municipal facilities. Under the leadership of Holger Cahill, who was not inclined to judge the art's "quality," the FAP engendered progressive experimentation and offered public art demonstrations, classes, and lectures (McKinzie 1973: xi; Park and Markowitz 1984: 178).

Two other important New Deal art programs were administered by the Treasury Department. From 1935 to 1939 the Treasury Relief Art Project (TRAP) employed artists, mostly those on relief, to decorate federal buildings whose construction was then managed by the Treasury. The second program was the Section of Fine Arts (initially named the Section of Painting and Sculpture), spurred by Edward Bruce's suggestion in 1934 that for each new federal building constructed, one percent of the total cost be set aside for its "embellishment." Under the leadership of Bruce (himself a painter and pragmatic administrator), Edward Rowan (another painter), and art critic Forbes Watson, the Section flourished until its closure in 1943. It commissioned individual artists for particular jobs, and offered anonymous competitions that "discovered" new talent (Prokopoff 1981: 78). The Section's decisions were not based on financial need, and rather than foster the collectivism of the FAP, its artists often continued in their private studio lives. Bruce insisted on aesthetic and technical standards in keeping with "good" art, convinced that exposure to such would enrich the quality of American life (McKinzie 1973: xi; Park and Markowitz 1984: 178). Thus the Section promoted more conventional styles that would not be off-putting to uninitiated eyes. As Marlene Park and Gerald Markowitz observe, the Section's "goal was to create a

4

contemporary American art, neither academic nor avant-garde, but based on experience and accessible to the general public" (1992: 136). Through projects such as post office murals, the Section not only underscored the federal government's presence in communities large and small, but brought art into the realm of the everyday with recognizable subjects depicted through familiar means.

Perhaps the New Deal programs demonstrated not so much public support for the arts, as public endorsement of economic relief (Mankin 1982: 118, 136). Though Netzer is correct that in retrospect the New Deal is too often idealized as a "happy marriage of big government and the arts" (1978: 54), it did have lasting effects. The New Deal affirmed art's importance in a democratic society, built a significant national collection of public artworks, nurtured creative energies that might have otherwise perished, and laid the groundwork for federal arts funding. As characterized by Jonathan Harris, the New Deal programs also politicized culture within specifically populist terms, projecting an image of "social utopia" to be achieved through capitalist means. Stereotypes of the modern artist as an aloof loner or self-interested recluse were replaced with notions of the "productive worker" and "good citizen," loyal to the nation (1995: 4, 8–10). New Deal artworks were also intended to cultivate national pride in a shared culture, while buttressing belief in a faltered economy. Park and Markowitz write:

> The New Deal sought to change the relationship between the artist and society by democratizing art and culture. Art project officials wrote that the mass of people were "underprivileged in art," and they endeavored to make art available to all … projects were a uniquely American blend, combining an elitist belief in the value of high culture with the democratic ideal that everyone in society could and should be the beneficiary of such efforts. (1992: 131–2)

Thus there was a pronounced strain of cultural democracy in the New Deal: for the first time all citizens, regardless of their educational background, socio-economic class, or geographical region, were entitled to have art in their daily lives (Park and Markowitz 1984: xvii, 5, 181). Embedded in the New Deal were a multitude of evocative tensions that directly influenced the future of American public art. Among these was the massive entity of a federal government, attending to state, municipal, and individual needs; and the desire to make "high"-minded ideals accessible to the "average" person, while forging a cohesive cultural identity. The experimental nature of the programs was tempered by more conservative, "middle-of-the-road" aesthetics; frictions occurred between nationalist rhetoric and regionalist tastes, and the aim to provide for citizens' material necessities while also enriching their cultural lives. Ironically, these goals were manifested through socialist strategies called upon to shore up American capitalism. These supposed contradictions are instructive for a populist treatment of public art, as they attest to the need for nuance and negotiation. Rather than dealing in absolutes, public art strives to reconcile popular will and collective aspirations with governmental oversight, private business, or the individual artist's vision. But one might ask if such compromise necessarily leads to conventional ends as suggested by the Section's agenda, or if it can offer challenges and provocation as had the FAP. Although the FAP remains the best-known New Deal art initiative, it was actually the Treasury Department's programs that provided direct lineage for the next phase of federally sponsored art patronage in the US, the Art-in-Architecture program of the General Services Administration.

General Services Administration's Art-in-Architecture Program

The groundwork for the Art-in-Architecture (A-i-A) program was laid in 1934, when Edward Bruce recommended that one percent of new federal building costs be earmarked for the commission of art. Eventually this proposal was implemented through the General Services Administration (GSA), the agency that oversees federal construction projects, and was made manifest with A-i-A's inception in 1963. Often referred to as "percent-for-art," A-i-A specified that up to one half of one percent of total construction costs for new federal buildings (later to include their repairs and alterations as well) be utilized to purchase contemporary works by American artists. The program was suspended in 1966 in response to inflated construction costs, and flack over Robert Motherwell's *New England Elegy* (JFK Building, Boston), a large Abstract Expressionist painting some people interpreted literally as a death scene. A-i-A was revived in 1972 under the Nixon administration, and since has provided consistent government arts patronage. In 1973 A-i-A began soliciting input from "expert" review panels convened by the National Endowment for the Arts (NEA) to avoid questions about the rigor of its selection process, which favored the wishes of project architects (Balfe and Wyszomirski 1987: 23–4). Yet the GSA retains final authority over artist selection and commission, rendering it a major taste-maker for American public art. Though the GSA has widely disseminated some excellent artworks, A-i-A projects range in quality and efficacy. Perhaps the most enduring effects of these efforts are not found in the physical works themselves, but in the public's greater awareness of public art, and the GSA's heightened sensitivity to the intricacies of placing it.

A-i-A helped solidify several philosophical precepts about the nature and function of public art in the US. The first is a simple assertion that truly "public" art should be literally *owned* by the citizens. Although commissioned by a federal agency, A-i-A artworks are understood to be property of the people, even when these might not accurately reflect prevailing tastes or engage the full comprehension of intended audiences. At times such art falls shy of the public's appreciation, especially when it shirks emotional and intellectual accessibility. Nonetheless, the general public's physical access to and ownership of art was cultivated, and a federally sponsored collection was amassed. Another philosophical current embedded in the A-i-A program is the (albeit gradual) recognition that public spaces and artworks are not interchangeable. The notion of a *site-sensitive* art, in which the particular location is taken into consideration, gained great currency as A-i-A became more conscious of placing artworks in hospitable spaces. This eventually led to *site-specific* approaches, in which the interaction between site and art is a prime determinant in the work's conception, design, and execution, with the art sometimes altering the site. The individual character of respective artworks and sites was increasingly acknowledged, and artists were more frequently commissioned to respond to particular places. Instead of glorified decorators sprucing things up at a project's end, artists consulted more often in the early planning stages.

A-i-A's percent-for-art formula subsequently became the model for many state and municipal art programs that also draw funds from construction budgets, and place art in sites such as schools and parks. In 1959 Philadelphia passed the first municipal percent-for-art ordinance in the US, followed next by Baltimore (1964), San Francisco (1967), and Seattle (1973). Hawaii became the first state to follow suit and adopted its percent-for-art policy in 1967. Yet, it would be misleading to say that the GSA consistently brought an enlightened approach to public art processes. Many A-i-A artists had little effect upon their sites' overall design, often commissioned to "formulate solutions compatible with an extant architectural conception" (Prokopoff 1981: 79). Some A-i-A works remain vigorously scrutinized by critics bemoaning the unfortunate proliferation of "plop art," guided by an "unstated assumption that a successful museum or gallery artist would be a successful public artist" (Senie 1992b: 230). Dubbed "turds in the plaza" by architect James Wines, such art is typified by the lone, epic, abstract sculpture, resting awkwardly in but unrelated to its vast surroundings. Its life being granted through percent-for-art dicta rather than an understanding of shared public culture, "plop art" cannot be saved by its egalitarian ambitions.

Although the GSA has aspired to greater outreach and consensus-building in the last few decades, emphasizing regional representation on selection panels and organizing meetings for artists and community members to discuss potential sites and local history, its heritage is still marked by some autocratic decision-making. The most enduring example of such was its 1979 commission of *Tilted Arc*, a 73-ton, 12-foot-high, 120-foot-long curved expanse of Cor-Ten steel, which self-oxidizes to yield a rusty patina. Artist Richard Serra conceived the work for its specific site, Federal Plaza (Jacob K. Javits Building, New York City), using pedestrian traffic patterns to determine both its form and placement. In 1989, eight years after its installation, *Tilted Arc* was dismantled under the cover of night. (Although this was authorized by the GSA's Acting

Administrator, Dwight Ink, it was Regional Administrator William Diamond who pushed for the *Arc*'s removal.) It remains in storage indefinitely. Complaints about the work's aesthetic impoverishment (a brooding, corroded "wall"), impediment of the space's "social use" (open space in Manhattan being a precious commodity), and spoiling effect on the surrounding environment (supposedly it lured graffiti, litter, rats, and criminals into the plaza) were touted as the impetus for its "departure." In actuality, an even wider matrix of factors came into play. Countless articles and numerous books have debated the *Arc*'s relative merits and weaknesses and the legal battles over its removal, so a protracted account is unnecessary here. But that the *Arc* persists to remind us of a federal agency overstepping its boundaries (at least from the art world's perspective) is essential.

According to Serra, *Tilted Arc* was designed to forge social function from sculptural space, and visually link various governmental buildings. The artist hoped to reorient visitors' perceptual relationships, to "dislocate or alter the decorative function of the plaza and actively bring people into the sculpture's context" (Serra qtd. in Doss 1995: 32). But critics argued that Serra subjugated the plaza in servitude to his sculpture, being more concerned with physical rather than social context (McConathy 1987: 11–12). Steven Dubin suggests no "overt message" accounted for *Tilted Arc*'s problems, but rather it was Serra's aesthetic choices, "whose artful qualities eluded" the public (1992: 25). Described as a "sullen blade," "eyesore," and "iron curtain" (Senie 1984: 52; Danto 1987: 90), to some viewers the *Arc* was overbearing and even menacing. Harriet Senie writes: "There was no way to avoid it; one became, willingly or not, a participant (not a spectator) in a city where staying uninvolved was … the preferred way to negotiate a public space" (2002: xiv). Thomas Hine concludes that *Tilted Arc* was "a great work of art," but the "qualities that gave it its power were precisely those that made it difficult to live with every day" (2001: 41).

Serra's emphasis on site-specificity transformed the act of removal into one of destruction for those critical of the GSA's practices. This claim gains credence in light of several facts. Serra's previous work was well known, and the GSA sought him out for a permanent piece (Serra received verbal assurances confirming this; Buskirk 1991: 43). After exhaustive project evaluation and approving detailed plans specifying scale, placement, and material, which included revisions made per the GSA's request, Serra was awarded the contract. The GSA knew what it was getting from Serra; as Robert Hughes snapped: "It did not expect a cute bronze of Peter Pan" (1985: 78). Finally, the GSA had troubled commissions in its recent past, most notably George Sugarman's *Baltimore Federal* (1975–7), which a US District judge described as a "security threat" despite its bright colors, whimsical abstract forms, and provision of seating. Though the A-i-A program was temporarily halted and an internal review conducted (Balfe and Wyszomirski 1987: 24), Sugarman's work remained in place, thanks to a mobilized art community, and the local press and people (Lewis 1977: 40; Thalacker 1980: 8–13; Senie 1992b: 176–7). As proven by the Baltimore case, "understanding is not instant" (Allen 1985: 248), yet the GSA did little to enhance public receptivity toward *Tilted Arc* before its installation. A small scale model of the work that "gave little real notion of the size and impact of the full piece" was placed in the GSA building's lobby, while a pole-and-string stakeout on the plaza offered no "accurate impression of the mass and solidity of the artwork itself" (Balfe and Wyszomirski 1987: 25). The GSA also did little to address resentment toward the work after its installation (Storr 1989: 276), which may have been intensified by poor working conditions at the site (McConathy 1987: 4). Though it can take years for an intended audience to acclimate to an artwork, and for a commissioning agency to evaluate the public's reactions (Grant 1989: 82), the GSA was anxious to cut bait.

The tribulations of *Tilted Arc* made their way to the general press, with publications like *People Weekly* portraying the work as a conspiracy between the federal government and art elite against the "people" (Carlson 1985: 138). But Serra's supporters perceived no such alliance between government and the art world. Instead they saw something insidious in the GSA's actions, believing that *Tilted Arc*'s removal was not actually motivated by the will of a deeply offended public, but by political aspirations, especially those of zealous GSA Regional Administrator William Diamond, who entered the scene three years after the work was installed. Since the GSA covers all design, execution, and installation costs, the agency maintains propriety rights over the works it commissions, and retains final authority over artwork removal or relocation. Prompted in particular by the complaints of Chief Justice Edward D. Re, Diamond circulated petitions and convened a *Tilted Arc* hearing, claiming to carry out the public's wishes. Diamond presided over the hearing and personally selected a five-member panel to hear testimony, none of whom were experts on public art. The hearing was to determine whether or not *Tilted Arc* should remain *in situ* – that is, in its original, intended location – or be relocated, though as Robert Storr observes, the hearing seemed little more than "parliamentary niceties" providing "camouflage for a fixed agenda" (1989: 273). While some members of the public decried the piece upon its installation, it remains unclear if they were still as upset by the time of the March 1985 hearing. Only 58 people bothered to testify against *Tilted Arc*, though there were more than 10,000 employees at Federal Plaza then, in addition to any other concerned citizens (Serra 1989: 36–7; Weyergraf-Serra and Buskirk 1991: 23, 57). Two-thirds of those who testified at the hearing, and the majority of those who wrote the GSA in regard to the matter, were in favor of keeping the work in situ (Senie 1989: 299). Yet Diamond's hearing concluded the piece would be removed, although the *Arc* was supposed to remain on the plaza until an alternative location was found. Diamond's detractors maintain he was predisposed against the work and manipulated public opinion and the media, creating what Serra characterized as an "imagined majority," to have the piece destroyed (1989: 37–8). The possibility of relocation was a moot point. While venues like Storm King Art Center expressed interest in hosting *Tilted Arc* they were unwilling to do so without the artist's consent, and Serra indicated he would disclaim authorship if the piece were installed elsewhere (Weyergraf-Serra and Buskirk 1991: 133). Though Hughes quipped that "the world is full of formerly 'site-specific' art," which has "not died from being moved" (1985: 78), as Nick Kaye perceives site-specific work, to move it is to "*re-place* it, to make it *something else*" (2000: 2).

Tilted Arc prompts questions about democracy that extend beyond the impact of the American two-party political system on public art. (It was commissioned under Carter's liberal Demo-cratic administration, while its removal occurred in the wake of Reagan-era conservatism and was led by Diamond, a Republican political appointee.) Though Serra, who honed his skills working in steel mills as a young adult, acknowledges that there are situations in which "the people's needs and my needs could be mutually related," he disavows populism as "art defeating." He proclaims that attracting "a bigger audience has nothing to do with the making of art" (Serra qtd. in Senie 1984: 55), and contends that "*Tilted Arc* was never intended to – nor did it – speak for the United States Government" (1989: 43). To protect the work Serra sued in 1986 for violation of his contract, free speech, and due process (McConathy 1987: 14), though his complaint and appeal were subsequently dismissed. When testifying at the 1985 hearing, Victor Ganz, then chair of the Battery Park City fine arts committee, implored the GSA to "have the courage to be elitist enough to be truly democratic" (Ganz qtd. in Howarth 1985: 99). But like Ganz, many of those who spoke in Serra's favor (as well as the NEA panel members who concluded removal of the *Arc* was tantamount to its destruction), are fairly categorized as art world "insiders." Were these people truly representative of or concerned for the broader public, or were they answering a call of duty to defend one of their own, attempting to insulate the borders of "high art"? And in his insistence upon a site-specificity that privileged aesthetics, did Serra consider the rights of the public, or only his own? While we may never determine whether it was truly populist forces that removed *Tilted Arc*, or if the people's voices were actually quieted by powerful vigilante bureaucrats, Thomas Crow finds the GSA's claims to represent the public rooted in "a decidedly elitist presupposition about what such people can and cannot absorb" (1996: 148–9). Erika Doss concurs, arguing that the GSA appropriated a "populist tone" to skew "the democratic process." Thus "*Tilted Arc*'s removal had less to do with public autonomy than with GSA sovereignty," though she notes that it is too easy to blame "the state" or a "cultural elite" as such polarization eclipses the nuances of public life (1995: 33–4). Regardless, the controversy made two things clear: the commissioning and installation processes for *Tilted Arc* were "distinctly flawed" (Balfe and Wyszomirski 1987: 25), and the subsequent removal of public art calls for as much careful consideration as its initial placement.

Before *Tilted Arc*'s installation, the plaza was not a "little lunchtime oasis" (Carlson 1985: 138), but a fairly inhospitable place with undistinguished architecture and a broken fountain (Crow 1996: 148). As described by Hughes, Federal Plaza was "one of the ugliest public spaces in America" (1985: 78). Immediately after the *Arc*'s removal a gaggle of standard-issue benches and planters were placed there, until the plaza required major structural work and the GSA folded an art initiative into its repairs budget. The agency "unilaterally" selected Martha Schwartz, who in 1997 furnished the space with more standard-issue benches (but this time acid-green ones arranged in serpentine patterns), which snake around mounds of earth (originally covered with grass, but since replanted with shrubs) occasionally spewing steam. On the Broadway side of the plaza now stands Beverly Pepper's *Sentinels* (1996), four abstract columns in that same rusty Cor-Ten steel. As Senie points out, there is more than a little irony here; though one can now sit and ignore the art more easily, there is no direct path across the plaza, which is still a place people rarely linger (2002: 96, 98–100, 102). In fact, both of the new works lack the strong presence of Serra's piece; Schwartz's design is playful in an ordinary way (colors and curves must be fun!), while Pepper's slender, vertical sculptures can escape notice altogether. Serra did not necessarily make Federal Plaza any prettier with *Tilted Arc*, nor did he make the pedestrian's commute any shorter or view any clearer. But he did make the space interesting. One of the most essential services the public artist can provide is to activate a space, which is precisely what Serra did for Federal Plaza, both physically and socially. Crow suggests that given the site's symbolism as a seat of federal authority, and its proximity to downtown art neighborhoods, one could anticipate that *Tilted Arc* would come "under extraordinary scrutiny in both its civic and aesthetic manifestations." But he also insists the plaza is permanently marked by "the shared memory of the trauma of the sculpture's removal" (Crow 1996: 144, 150). *Tilted Arc*'s fate has become the key to its lasting value; unable to stay in its intended home, the dialogue it fosters extends its lifespan in perpetuity. Crow concludes:

Large questions concerning the relations between public symbols and private ambitions, between political freedom, legal obligations

13

and aesthetic choice, have been put vividly and productively into play by the work, engendering debates that might have been abstract and idle had it not existed – and which might have been complacently put aside had it gone on existing. (1996: 150)

Among continued hesitations about A-i-A is that it expects art-works like *Tilted Arc* to rehabilitate poorly designed architecture or unwelcoming public spaces and provide amenities, even when artists make no claims to do so. Patricia Phillips suggests that percent-for-art programs often lead to a "minimum basic standard" that ultimately begets mediocrity and thwarts creative potential (1988: 93). But as director of the Arts for Transit program (responsible for placing public art in New York's subway system), Wendy Feuer questioned the appropriateness of governmental funding for confrontational works. Though Feuer acknowledged the desirability of challenging art experiences, she recognized their increased vulnerability in widely accessible public settings (1989: 139–40, 145, 148, 153). Almost any percent-for-art initiative has the capacity to generate controversy; works are aimed at audiences that might have "no particular interest in art" and placed where one "can't really avoid them." Alan Ehrenhalt proposes that such programs fare better when they involve "ordinary people who will be the front-line consumers day in and out." While he admits such measures could not guarantee "better artistic decisions, or even necessarily different ones," he asserts there is much to gain in giving the public a voice about matters on its own turf (1994: 9–10). After the *Tilted Arc* debacle, the A-i-A selection process seemed more thoughtful and even tentative, and the GSA made earlier outreach efforts to "local communities which are to be recipients of the art" (Ted Weiss qtd. in Howarth 1985: 98). Yet we should not encourage the GSA to reduce public art to a "popularity contest." As Senie reminds us: "Controversy is loud and appreciation often silent and unmeasurable" (1992b: 230). Clearly, matters of taste cannot, and ought not, be legislated. The management of government sponsorship, art world sentiments, and public relations is not a task for the diplomatically challenged.

National Endowment for the Arts' Art-in-Public-Places Program

In 1965 the National Endowment for the Arts was founded under Johnson's administration, marking the first time in American history that substantial federal tax-based funds were allocated for arts spending at the state and local levels (Katz 1984: 28). In doing so the arts were "*officially* sanctioned as significant contributors to our nation's well-being" (Smagula 1983: 13), and "support for culture" was established as "a legitimate government responsibility" (Buchwalter 1992: 1). At its core, NEA policy emphasizes the dissemination of and access to art experiences regardless of any perceived social barriers, and the agency of culture's receivers; providing the individual with an opportunity to make an "educated choice" about having "high quality" art in one's life. Thus the Endowment often finds itself straddling expectations for high culture and hopes for populist appeal (Wyszomirski 1982: 13–14; Arian 1989: 5–6), in an effort to provide "quality" art for "everybody." To that end the NEA established its Art-in-Public-Places (A-i-P-P) program in 1967, which intended to reach the widest possible audiences by responding to local requests. Its official aims included: increasing awareness of contemporary art; fostering aesthetic enhancement and socially-minded redevelopment of public spaces; offering American artists, especially emerging ones, opportunities to work in public contexts; supporting artistic experimentation; and engendering direct community involvement in the commission and placement of art. According to Brian O'Doherty, a former director of the NEA's Visual Arts Programs, A-i-P-P signaled "a crucial change in perspective which removed the idea of the Federal Government imposing art works on communities that had no option but to accept or reject them" (1974: 44).

In John Beardsley's estimation, A-i-P-P was one of the government's most visible and at moments, controversial, art programs. Instead of explicating definitive standards by which to judge the qualitative merits of art, A-i-P-P adopted a self-consciously democratic process open to scrutiny and debate, and courted audiences not necessarily predisposed to art appreciation (1981a: 9). While this program is the most egalitarian in spirit of those discussed in this chapter, its moniker, "art in public places," is a semantic gambit. It does not focus upon the content, audiences, or processes by which art might become public, but rather the physical places where such art is sited; "artworks purchased or commissioned for publicly owned or publicly accessible spaces. It is art made public, outside the home or museum" (Beardsley 1981b: 43; Allen 1985: 246). While definitions of "public place" are mutable, it seems easier to arrive at some agreement over these than to concur about what constitutes "public art." As Jerry Allen observed, the terms "public" and "art" are inherently contradictory. To modernist sensibilities, art was "individual inquiry" rather than actions on behalf of a collective body, marking a tension that estranged "the public for whose benefit the artwork" was placed (1985: 246). A-i-P-P labored to counter this rift with proactive community initiatives that would develop public space as "a symbol of a neighborhood's vitality and character," instead of "an emblem of its disorganization and poverty of spirit" (Schwartz 2000: 13). To do so, A-i-P-P encouraged citizens to take responsibility for and ownership of such spaces, including raising financial resources. A-i-P-P did not solicit grant applicants but provided matching federal funds to support community-sponsored projects, which originated from ad-hoc groups, cultural organizations, nonprofits, and local governmental or art agencies. Thus projects were financed through mixes of municipal, corporate, federal, and private sources. While this matrix of involved parties sparked rich dialogue and emphasized shared goals, it also underscored the pluralism of American society. With so many interests and values represented, an A-i-P-P project offered no single expected outcome.

In 1966 the National Council for the Arts pilot-tested the idea for A-i-P-P; by 1967 the program's initial grants were made under the leadership of Henry Geldzahler, the NEA's Visual Arts Programs' inaugural director. The first A-i-P-P work, *La Grande Vitesse*, an immense, bright red steel sculpture by Alexander Calder, then one of America's preeminent living artists, was placed in Grand Rapids, Michigan (commissioned 1967, installed 1969). Initially decried mostly because of its abstraction, *La Grande Vitesse* eventually became "a cultural sign of a decidedly upscale urban identity," a "civic logo" that appeared on everything from the city's letterhead to its garbage trucks (Senie 1992b: 219). The sculpture ushered in a wave of art enthusiasm in the community; although it may not have suited everyone's taste, the citizens of Grand Rapids (a city not previously known for its art) were proud to have a major artwork by an important artist in their hometown. At this early stage, A-i-P-P's goals were fairly modest: find an eminent artist whose work could "provide a commanding focus point" for a substantial plaza (Beardsley 1981a: 16–17). There was little concern for context, message, or site-specificity. Yet as Senie posits, this first commission was instructive; *La Grande Vitesse* was not a substitute for urban renewal, but part of a larger initiative toward such (1992b: 219). Seattle received the second A-i-P-P grant for Isamu Noguchi's *Black Sun* (installed 1969), a 9-foot-tall circle of black granite, pierced in the middle and covered with irregularly shaped outcroppings. Seattle quickly embraced art as a vital component of its comprehensive revitalization efforts. The city established a standing A-i-P-P committee, brought artists in at planning stages, and composed juries of art professionals and community members to select its public artworks (Beardsley 1981a: 20–3; Allen 1985: 244–5).

With time, the nature of A-i-P-P shifted toward greater public involvement; instead of focusing on masterworks by famous artists, it took a "chat them up" approach to the community (Raven 1989: 11, 15). By 1973 the program had formalized guidelines, but it was the 1979 revision of operations that greatly enhanced community accountability for the projects. While the NEA continued to provide assistance for proposals and grant applications, it abolished its joint panel system. This effectively removed the NEA from artist selections, requiring communities to develop their own criteria and procedures. An interested party, following NEA guidelines, had to initiate and carry through a commission: selecting the artist and site; raising matching funds; building support from local officials and neighborhood members; and ultimately assuming responsibility for the artwork's installation and maintenance. The NEA does not own the art, its sponsoring community or organization does. Although Judith Balfe and Margaret Wyszomirski feel A-i-P-P shared a primarily aesthetic purpose with A-i-A (1987: 22–3),

17

I suggest that A-i-P-P's efforts were characterized by a more distinctly pronounced social dimension, emphasizing public inclusion from the program's start. A-i-P-P's approach was essential in fostering acceptance of its artworks. The projects often incorporated content relevant to their local audiences rather than addressing generalized ones, frequently offered utilitarian or rehabilitative functions, and relied upon sustained commitments from the public. Thus there was a notable distinction between A-i-A, which is federally sponsored but offers limited opportunities for public involvement, and A-i-P-P, which provided partial government funding but depended on extensive community participation (Beardsley 1981a: 9–13; 1981b: 44–5).

The egalitarian idealism underlying A-i-P-P's precepts is not without its challenges. For example, Miami Dade County, frequently cited as one of the most successful municipal offshoots of the NEA's A-i-P-P, still had its share of troubles. Miami Dade instituted its own A-i-P-P program in 1973, earmarking a percent and a half of construction funds for art commissions. In its heyday the Miami Dade program boasted an array of educational and outreach initiatives, and commissioned high-profile artists who executed works that garnered critical and public praise. Yet the program had difficulty sustaining support from local politicians and officials. The aura of "civic pride" that had ushered it in waned with the County's economic woes in the 1980s. Collection of mandated funds and utilization of potential sites were hampered by various parties, reminding us that the County is comprised of multiple publics, all of whom are not necessarily in sympathy with A-i-P-P objectives. If this "first public" of bureaucrats and contractors cannot be won over, the art never gains broader audiences (Joselit 1990: 142–51, 183). Without securing steady sources of political and financial capital, the livelihood of any art program is, at best, vulnerable.

Today the NEA's A-i-P-P program no longer exists, and the health of the Endowment is tenuous. The NEA was battered in the late 1980s and 1990s by neoconservative forces that gained steam in the Reagan era (the President suggested eliminating both the NEA and National Endowment for the Humanities altogether; Dubin 1992: 281). Led by Senator Jesse Helms, who proposed a ban on "obscene and indecent art," right-wingers made dramatic incursions on the vision and funding of the NEA, adopting a "pseudopopulist stance," which ironically purported to preserve public culture by exercising tighter control over it (Doss 1995: 27–8). Though efforts to abolish the NEA were unsuccessful and the Endowment was reauthorized in 1997, it is a shadow of its formerly robust self. The Endowment no longer awards grants to individual artists in most cases, and Congress can intervene more directly in the NEA's selection of artists and distribution of monies. And of course, the NEA remains under the federal government's control; its director is a presidential appointee, and its continued funding is dependent upon Congress. Though George Yudice acknowledges conservativism's corrosive effect on the NEA, he suggests that the Endowment's gradual erosion is indicative of the government's withdrawal from arts patronage in general. This is coupled with an increased emphasis on the "utility and relevance" of the arts, which are expected to serve civic, social, and educational ends that justify their support, rather than a "humanistic tenet" that provides "uplift, a safe haven for freedom or inner vision." Yet the NEA has made an enduring mark on the landscape of American public art. By 1980 all 50 states had their own arts agencies, a proliferation likely stimulated by the NEA and its former chair, Nancy Hanks, as only four states had such agencies before 1965 (Yudice 1999: 18, 20, 25–7, 29).

In 1991 the NEA proposed to combine the A-i-P-P and Visual Artists Forums funding categories; by 1993 these were indeed merged. The last proposals that received A-i-P-P grants often empha- sized "social problems and multiculturalism," and "the social situa- tion of a site" (Senie 2002: 108). Today "public art" proposals to the NEA are channeled to its Grants for Arts Projects categories: usually Access to Artistic Excellence, which seeks to "provide access to the arts for all Americans"; or Challenge America: Reaching Every Community Fast-Track Review, which offers smaller grants more quickly to "underserved populations." (Education-based grants are available through the Learning in the Arts for Children and Youth program; arts.endow.gov 2007.) One wonders if these programs can sustain initiative and collaboration at the community level, and rep- resent the complex multiplicity of any given population, as A-i-P-P had tried to do. A-i-P-P was far from perfect, but it prompted local communities to claim their own spaces and excavate their own histories in order to "define and redefine themselves" (Breitbart and Worden 1993: 27–8). Will the next generation of NEA programs knit neighborhoods together in shared visions for their futures? Or will they proffer simplified solutions to society's ills that alienate members of the public? Ultimately, what will be best served: a federal agenda, art world interests, or the communities who live with the art?

A problematic that unifies the New Deal, Art-in-Architecture, and Art-in-Public-Places programs is that their understandings of "public art" were frequently predicated upon physical accessibility. If art was in a space to which the audience gained entry without paying a fee (or if that fee was paid to utilize infrastructure or transportation services, not to view art), it was "public." But such a reductive definition negates the truly public aspects of art; its ability to stimulate the intellects, senses, and emotions of viewers regardless of location. When Phillips contends "the public dimension is a psychological, rather than a physical or environmental construct" (1988: 93), she recognizes that art for "the people" must not necessarily be set in their daily paths, but needs to engage their hearts, incite their minds, and risk some discontent along the way. It is this last point that underscores the great shortcoming of much government-sponsored public art: the desire to propagate good will and nurture consensus has cultivated an aesthetics of the bland. Unlikely to offend many viewers, the most probable peril of such art is that of boring its audience. Even the earliest public artworks commissioned by our government had the potential for controversy. Horatio Greenough's colossal portrait of *George Washington* (1832–41) was met with disdain; some viewers found the President clothed in a Roman toga too undignified and revealing (Mankin 1982: 116–17). But to elevate official sponsorship above the level of "dull interior design bought from a tax-deductible art budget" (Miles 1989: 7), the government must welcome the discord that likely comes with art patronage (Levitt 1991: 20). Erika Doss rightly insists that controversy is "healthy and hopeful," maintaining that "fierce debate" about public art "is a sign that Americans still hold out for the possibilities of culture democracy" (1995: vii–viii, 14–15).

Writing in the midst of the *Tilted Arc* controversy, Peter Blake bemoaned the quality of art created through "universal suffrage" in which theoretically "every taxpayer has the right to vote on its form, content, site, and the selection of its creator" (1987: 286). Likewise, artist Robert Morris lamented "populist" government art policies, which appease the "middle-brow" with "mediocre" art, diffuse "concentrated culture," deflate the avant-garde, and seize upon the entertainment value of art (1992: 251). It is true that a good deal of substandard art has been produced and placed through the patronage of our government, but there has also been work of great substance that interrogates established aesthetic and social ideals. Morris too lightly dismissed the transformative power of being entertained; the avant-garde is not so fragile as to be threatened by some levity, and providing amusement and enjoyment are meaningful goals. Inviting more people to engage in public art processes will require tactful negotiation, and at times acquiescence, but such concessions could be worthwhile if formerly disenfranchised individuals gain personal stakes in the arts. Although short-lived, the Artist Project of the Comprehensive Employment Training Act (CETA) was a government-sponsored arts program that was populist both in intent and in approach. Begun under the Carter administration, the Artist Project enabled thousands of American artists to offer free performances, teach classes, and make public art, usually in "close communication and ... collaboration with grassroots community groups," thus forging a dialogue "between artists ... and nonartists, who very likely had never had contact with artists in any capacity before" (Maksymowicz 1990: 149–50). We cannot overlook the shared legacy of the New Deal, A-i-A, and A-i-P-P, each of which made claims for the *social* functions of art. Not relegated solely to self-reflexive aesthetic concerns, artworks increasingly reflected cultural values, responded to political issues, and directly engaged their audiences in critical dialogues of the day. By the end of the twentieth century social context could not be ignored in the practices of public art. A greater recognition of and appreciation for the forces of populism had finally arrived.

Chapter 2   Conventional Wisdom: Populist Intentions within Established Paradigms

The history of art has sometimes been presented as a history of styles. The history of public art will more likely be seen as a history of intentions. (Miles 1989: 39)

As stated in Chapter 1, public art's basic criteria have often been delineated as follows: its works are designated for larger audiences, and placed to attract their attention; it intends to provide aesthetic experiences that edify, commemorate, or entertain; and its messages are comprehensible to generalized audiences. Historically American public art (although we are not alone in this) had frequently sifted into predictably reductive, overplayed categories such as the war monument, tribute portrait, or austere abstraction. These were usually "fittingly dignified" and "understandable but not innovative" (Doezema 1977: 18–19). Yet even when working within the conventional paradigms of public art, some artists have managed to enlarge and challenge such traditions instead of regurgitating formulaic "solutions," and tease out slippages between the "public" and "private." In doing so, these artists embody a more populist attitude. Some of their pieces are so completely absorbed into the surroundings they literally escape notice as "art"; they nudge at and whisper to us so that we perceive their effects in subtle ways. Other works scream for our attention; unwilling to be mitigated by site or circumstance, they insist we pay them mind.

Writing in 1988, Patricia Phillips complained that public art lacked "clear definitions," "constructive theory," or "coherent objectives" (1988: 93). While the public art field has grown immensely in the last 20 years, such definitions, theory, and objectives still elude us; by emphasizing the function of populist sensibilities in public art, these come into sharper focus, particularly the objectives. Many critics fear that populism engenders a flattening out of art, exchanging edginess for mass appeal, while awarding artists for public relations skills instead of daring. But two points must be emphasized here. First, accessibility is not the parent of mediocrity; one does not have to "dumb down" art or avoid challenging content to be accessible. Second, speaking concurrently *with* many potential publics, some specialized and others nonspecific, is quite different than talking *at* a single, monolithic audience. An accessible conversation is not necessarily simple-minded. This chapter examines how various artists interrogate the persistent conventions of public art; by no means is this an encyclopedic overview, but rather a populist lens through which to view and reorient our appreciation for such art. To this end, one need put aside preconceived notions and qualitative judgments centered on aesthetic issues, and consider that art is most fully public when it sincerely extends emotional and intellectual access to its viewers. This is not to say that aesthetics or physical accessibility does not matter, but that they are, at times, beside the point.

Art as Monument, Art as Memorial

A monument seeks to *celebrate*. It offers a physical manifestation to mark a military victory or depict a cultural hero, for example, and its tone is most often congratulatory and triumphant. A memorial aims to *commemorate*. Expressing loss from war or disease, or remembering a tragic or profound event, a memorial provides opportunities to reflect and grieve, and may or may not result in built form. In his study of Holocaust memorials, James Young defines the "art of public memory" as extending beyond aesthetics to include activities that bring memorials "into being, the constant give-and-take between memorials and viewers, and, finally, the responses of viewers to their own world in light of a memorialized past." Public memory also encompasses the "ebb and flow of public sentiment and will." Instead of a collective, monolithic memory, Young argues for "collected memory"; aggregate in construction, plural in meanings, and mutable in form and context. This "collected memory" is comprised of diverse and competing responses, some planned and others accidental, which shift with time, circumstance, and ideology as they converge at each site. Even when socially constructed values and a sense of common history are shared, he insists one's memories are unique and discrete. Thus, "neither a purely formal nor a historicist approach accommodates the many other dimensions at play in public monuments." Young concludes that memorial spaces are not permanent "witness-relics," but "forever incomplete" and "fundamentally interactive"; inert until visitors imbue them with memory (1992: 58, 69; 1993: viii–xii, 3, 6, 15).

Among his "10 Propositions" on modern public sculpture Albert Elsen observed there remained a need for memorials to perform conventional functions, but that the monument's nature had changed. Instead of glorifying a particular person or place, contemporary monuments focused on more generalized celebrations of "art and life" (1989b: 291). For example, the work of Claes Oldenburg caters to a broad public, employing recognizable objects from daily life, but challenging our preconceptions about these with witty plays on scale and material. Oldenburg was among the earliest members of the Pop Art movement, which sought to counter art world pretensions with vernacular subject matter. He rendered hard objects soft (*Ghost Typewriter* is essentially a floppy bean bag), and edible food indigestible (*Two Cheeseburgers with Everything* is cast in papier-mâché). In his hands modestly proportioned items became gigantic totems (a cherry-topped spoon acts as a human-scale bridge). But beyond these more obvious shifts, Oldenburg's works proffer subtle references and ironies for those seeking further analysis, as attested to by the multitude of conversations one can overhear in earshot of these. His *Clothespin* (1976), an enormous sculpture of the household item sited across the street from Philadelphia's City Hall, is available to viewers on multiple levels of recognition and inquiry. It is a quickly apprehended joke on the absurdity of a handheld object expanded to a height of 45 feet, or a commentary on the state of political affairs, gingerly held together. And it will eventually become a reminder of domesticity past, when people regularly hung out their wash. *Clothespin* also acknowledges the nearby Philadelphia Museum of Art's collection of Constantin Brancusi's sculpture, literally mimicking the reductive form and lovers' embrace in *The Kiss*. Through such multivalent readings, Oldenburg extends a wide invitation. His work is populist not only in form – working with familiar objects – but in intent and context. The artist does not impose a single interpretation upon some imagined homogenous audience, but keeps meaning free-flowing, without privileging one level of understanding over another.

Though many writers have scrutinized Maya Lin's *Vietnam Veterans Memorial* (1982), the work's ability to connect with wide and varied audiences deserves consideration here. Lin's commission came through an open competition, the guidelines of which stipulated that entries were to: be reflective and contemplative in nature; make no political statements; harmonize with the site (The Mall, Washington, DC); and include the names of Americans dead, missing, or captured as a result of the Vietnam War. Lin conceived a subdued minimalist form; two 240-foot walls bearing a painfully long list of 58,476 names. These are etched into polished black granite, which acts as a mirror reflecting images of the living upon names of the dead. Viewers literally descend into the earth, are engulfed by the names, and then rise up again. In a sense the memorial is both a massive tombstone and a scar attesting to our wounded past.

Tom Finkelpearl describes the *Veterans Memorial* as "both more personal and more abstract than the traditional memorial," imbued with "an aura of fact" (2001: 111). Lin's stated aim was to present the "facts" without dictating interpretation. But despite her efforts to avoid sentimentalism and political commentary, the memorial frankly lays bare the cost of war and the magnitude of its losses. Lin's work quietly sits in its corner plot, sunken into the ground, unlike its imposing neighbors on The Mall rising triumphantly into the air. The *World War II Memorial* designed by architect Friedrich St. Florian (2004) emphasizes victory, though it ironically resembles one of Albert Speer's starkly grand designs for Hitler. It also suggests that the war's scale dictated the size of its monument. Sited on a prime piece of The Mall, it attempts to forge collective remembrance of national history rather than offer an "art experience." Here a noisy, indeed festive, atmosphere is created by a jumbled conglomeration of fountains, sculpture, architecture, and text. People take pictures of themselves next to the "memorial" (I have never seen this occur at Lin's *Veterans Memorial*); another tourist site to check off the list. In contrast, Lin allows the unsettling, unfinished nature of the Vietnam War to persist. Despite its public setting, Lin conceived her memorial not as a "billboard," but as a "book" for intimate reading (Finkelpearl 2001: 121). This prompts individual contemplation, and her viewers respond with reverence, as if visiting a public cemetery of personal grief. Though Lin was purposefully subtle in her aesthetic choices (Lin 2005): simple type-face, reflective stone, dark hue, and a gradual descent into the ground; experienced together these are less than neutral. It is not these choices alone, but the mood of quiet meditation they evoke, and our ability to interact with the work, that accounts for the memorial's populist appeal.

Before Lin's work was installed it prompted great controversy. Veterans in particular were cynical about its supposedly anti-war sentiments, characterizing it as a "black ditch" and "An Asian Memorial for an Asian War" (Finkelpearl 2001: 118, 123). They were also skeptical about the artist, a female college student in her early twenties who had never fought in combat. Neoconservative forces headed by James Watt (then Secretary of the Interior) and Ross Perot (a wealthy businessman with his own political aspirations) succeeded in placing a more "traditional" monument just 100 feet away, though thankfully not at the apex of the *Vietnam Veterans Memorial* as was initially suggested. This is Frederick Hart's *Three Fighting Men* (1984), a representational bronze of over-life-size soldiers, primarily paid for by Perot. (In 1993 Glenna Goodacre's overly dramatic *Vietnam Women's Memorial* was installed nearby, which depicts two nurses attending a wounded GI, while a third keeps watch for a helicopter.) Hart's sculpture "lacks the emotional wallop" of Lin's memorial (Apgar 1992: 28), and receives far less attention. As Thomas Crow aptly noted, the "self-appointed defenders of popular virtue" wrongly assumed the public would find Lin's abstraction incomprehensible, when in fact it "exactly corresponds to the emotional needs of the 'average' mourners" (1996: 149). Lin's commission came about through the efforts of Jan Scruggs (a former army corporal), who established the Vietnam Veterans Memorial Committee. Though the memorial's siting on Washington's Mall required Congressional approval, it was paid for with private contributions, many from individual veterans and members of the public (Kelly 1996: 18). After its installation Lin's work was quickly embraced by "an unusually diverse public" (Miles 2004: 103), and remains enormously popular, being one of the most visited sites in Washington. (The universality of its language is confirmed by the proliferation of memorials that adopted its style in hopes of evoking similar responses.) Viewer reactions to the memorial, even above the artist's intent, attest to its publicness. Visitors regularly leave mementoes as they might at gravesites, and touch the memorial or make rubbings of the names, as though their loved ones' spirits reside here. Yet one does not need to have personally known someone named on the wall to be struck by the enormity of loss. Regardless of one's feelings about the war, Lin's memorial can be "profoundly moving" (Apgar 1992: 27).

W. J. T. Mitchell perceived a duality in Lin's work: "It can be experienced both as an object of national mourning and reconciliation that is absolutely inclusive, embracing and democratic, and as a critical parody and inversion of the traditional war memorial" (1990: 3). But in Michael Kelly's estimation, there is no parody here. He insists Lin's memorial offers a "politically astute" approach that considers Americans' ambivalence toward this war, and thus wisely seeks no consensus (1996: 19–20). The artist suggests her memorial is the "anti-monument" (Lin 2005), which is perhaps why it is able to elicit mourning for both national and personal losses. Lin's receipt of this prestigious commission is significant. Had entrants' identities been revealed during the jurying process it is unlikely that Lin – an Asian-American undergraduate studying architecture at Yale University – would have been selected. Yet she was an ideal choice for the job; rather than spouting personal beliefs or letting "specific politics ... get in the way of looking at the sacrifices made by individual veterans," she focused on "the human response" to and "psychological understanding" of war. Lin's impulses to avoid sensationalism, invite personal interaction, and trust "the viewer to think" without leading her to specific conclusions (Lin qtd. in Finkelpearl 2001: 116, 119) are consummately populist ones. Young observed that "in the absence of shared beliefs or common interests" memorials can "lend a common spatial frame to otherwise disparate experiences and understandings" of a "fragmented populace" (1993: 6–7). Lin's *Vietnam Veterans Memorial* has accomplished precisely that, allowing visitors to share in a resonant experience rather than a single memory.

Art as Amenity

After decades of complaints that much "public art" had little to do with the public, art's functionality gained a renewed emphasis, with street furniture becoming standard public art fare. Such utilitarianism held particular appeal for Americans, characterized as indigenously pragmatic (Doezema 1977: 14). As Harriet Senie asserts, the public is often an "involuntary audience" for public art, forced to negotiate a seemingly hostile or incomprehensible "foreign object" intruding upon its "familiar turf " (1992a: 240). Conversely, while waiting for a bus, one appreciatively sits on a nearby bench, usually unconcerned with who made it or any other functions it might serve. Despite David Joselit's lament that "artist-designed furniture" can beget "bland practice that relegates artists to the role of superior park-bench designers" (1989: 131), that conceived by Scott Burton avoids banality without compromising distinctive style. The furniture he placed in city streets and neighborhood parks may frequently go unacknowledged by its users as "art," but this circumstance was acceptable to the artist. Perceptive of the distinctions and similarities between the utilitarian object and objet d'art, Burton produced work that was equally at home on a street and in a museum. Burton's sculpture-furniture was informed by his background as an art historian and critic who wished to speak plainly to audiences. In particular, he was influenced by Bauhaus designers like Marcel Breuer, who intended to make "good design" available to the public. Thus Burton made art welcoming instead of intimidating. For example, he transformed the self-reflexive condition of

Minimalist art into newfound social and utilitarian purposes. While maintaining Minimalism's "architectonic clarity," he also coaxed humanistic "charisma" and accessibility from his pristine shapes (R. Smith 1978: 138–9). The directness of Burton's form and function is certainly populist, especially as he opened up the interpretation of his works by seizing upon their double lives. Unornamented minimalist rhetoric is rendered in luxurious, meticulously worked materials. His pieces are publicly sited but profoundly intimate, meant to be experienced through direct, individual body contact. They are available to the passerby, yet only affordable to the wealthy collector. A chair is not just a chair but a representation of such, offering a tension between the sensual aesthetic object and the functional one. Burton was unwilling to let his work reside within the confines of categorical distinctions: furniture or art, private or public.

Some of Burton's most "public" works were sponsored by private patronage. His first corporate commission came from the Equitable Life Assurance Society of America, and highlights the coming together of private and public, corporate and cultural ambitions. Equitable Center (Equitable's new building was to connect to Paine Webber's; together they would occupy a full city block in midtown Manhattan) attested to the rise of "privately owned public spaces" like hotel and office lobbies. In New York these were spurred by "incentive zoning" instituted in 1961, which offered floor area bonuses and zoning concessions to developers providing public spaces. As planner Jerold Kayden admits, not all privately owned public spaces are well designed, inviting, or as accessible as they are legally obligated to be. But when they are mindfully conceived, as was the attempt at Equitable Center, they can forge lively, interactive places (2000). Equitable Center was budgeted at 200 million dollars with over 7 million earmarked for the purchase and commission of artwork. This vast art program was a public relations move, and an attempt to enhance the real estate value and marketability of the site (Stephens 1986: 118). But the powers that be at Equitable were neither uninterested in art, nor reduced it to decorative baubles. Expected to serve as an aesthetic and social fix, art was to make the site more palatable to the "right kind of people" and less interesting to the "wrong kind." Of course, this notion is deeply flawed, both in premise and practice. While we can expect that

Equitable would seek to create an environment conducive to its business practices, profiling potential users seems at the very least distasteful. Yet Equitable is more egalitarian-spirited than many other private corporations, and cannot necessarily be asked to solve abiding social problems. According to Senie, we may rightfully regard corporate motives with "some skepticism," but their efforts do not inevitably result in poor public art. She concludes the "responsibility remains with the viewer to filter out the auxiliary advertising impact of the context" (1992b: 222).

Burton did work both inside and outside of Equitable Center. Indoors he provided the *Atrium Furnishment* (1986) for the lobby of the new tower, consulting with a curator from the Whitney Museum of American Art hired by Equitable. The *Furnishment* features a massive banquette fashioned from dark green marble and an arc-shaped tree bed, which curve around a water table with exotic plantings. Burton's rich materials and attention to detail evoke notions of prestige and quality, certainly desirable components of Equitable's corporate identity. His furniture helps mitigate the overwhelming scale and rectilinear design of the lobby, though an oversized mural by Roy Lichtenstein undermines some of its more meditative effects. Though *Atrium Furnishment* is aesthetically satisfying and quite useable, it is not as accomplished as Burton's outdoors pieces here, *Urban Plaza North* and *Urban Plaza South* (1985–6). The south plaza is appointed with a series of mushroom-like tables, each with three stools (Fig. 1). Although these seats have no backs or arms, which might make users feel vulnerable on a city street, their organization into tidy clusters imbues them with a sense of camaraderie, and their scale humanizes the cavernous spaces between skyscrapers. The sleek granite, a richly variegated green-gray, has held up well to the elements, and is inviting to the lunching workers who populate the tables in the warmer months. On the north plaza Burton provides opportunities for social interaction, though not as pronounced as on the south. He arranged his stone benches so their users are within visual and physical proximity of each other, but at odd angles and thus they do not necessarily face one another. The artist asks us to acknowledge others but does not force contact. Even when unoccupied, Burton's work retains an anthropomorphic presence, which continues to

Figure 1 Scott Burton. *Urban Plaza South*. 1985–6. Equitable Center, New York City. Photographer: Brooke A. Knight. © Estate of Scott Burton. Collection: AXA Financial.

enliven the spaces. Lucy Lippard once proclaimed that being "noticeable" is "a necessary prerequisite of public art" (1967/68: 230). On the street Burton's furniture-sculpture may not be recognizable to all as "art" but it is noticed and used by many, if primarily as a place to eat or rest one's feet. Corporate lobbies or museums are less likely to promote these amenity functions, but the context of a street tells us that it is okay to utilize Burton's civic-minded work, which encourages potential users to more freely negotiate relationships to it. In claiming the moniker of "public artist" Burton moved away from modernist conceptions of art as hermetic, to place art "not in front of but around, behind, underneath (literally) the audience in an *operational* capacity" (Burton qtd. in K. Johnson 1990: 161).

Though Burton noted that Equitable was amenable to him (Stephens 1986: 123), he was not asked to confer on matters of architectural planning. Yet he became convinced that artists should be involved throughout the conception of a space, and thus accepted an invitation to collaborate at the Massachusetts Institute of Technology (MIT). In addition to its percent-for-arts program, the school held a National Endowment for the Arts (NEA) matching grant for its Wiesner Building (1979–85), which was to house both arts and media technology programs. According to Wiesner project director Kathy Halbreich, the plan was to challenge the notion of "art in architecture" with an integrative approach that brought artists into the evolving design process (1984: 56). A visual arts committee and the architect, I. M. Pei, selected artists and assigned them particular "zones" in which to execute their work. The Wiesner project was marked by tensions, conflicting sensibilities, and successive rounds of give-and-take compromise between participants. Of the original six artists, only three stayed on: Richard Fleischner, who designed the exterior courtyard's paving, seating, and plantings; Kenneth Noland, who conceived color bands that enlivened the building's exterior and interior surfaces; and Burton, who focused on the interior's stairway, railings, and lobby furnishings. Burton's *Atrium Arc Seating and Railings* (1985) are so thoroughly integrated with the building they could be overlooked, yet their forms prompted Pei to modify his original design for the interior balconies. But despite the image of a "nonhierarchical creative union," Pei and his associates clearly wielded the most power (Graves 1993).

At Battery Park City (BPC), a waterside redevelopment project in New York City (see Chapter 6), the power balance was more equal. Burton joined forces with fellow artist Siah Armajani, architect Cesar Pelli, and landscape architect M. Paul Friedberg to collaboratively design a vast plaza fronting the World Financial Center (the BPC's largest public space). Armajani's contributions may be the most conspicuous; railings bearing quotations about New York by Walt Whitman and Frank O'Hara. But Burton's *Granite Benches*, whose curvature echoes the water's edge, seem most used. (His *Plaza Seating*, a grouping of tables, chairs, and steps, is too diminutive in the space.) No doubt this art-as-amenity can get lost in its environment, leading Peter Boswell to decry the "common banality" of "art by committee," typified by such plazas (1991). But Ken Johnson found the BPC plaza a welcome relief: "It doesn't muscle you with the authoritative rhetoric of the premodern monument; it doesn't flaunt an ostentatious individuality; and it doesn't nag you in the ideologically corrective way of the contemporary activist public art" (1990: 219). Burton once remarked that his work was "a rebuke to the art world," which had neglected its social responsibilities (Burton qtd. in Princenthal 1987: 131). Though some might complain that his art was too expensive or subtle to be truly public, Nancy Princenthal maintains that Burton was genuinely populist: he enhanced the relationship between art and life without being conciliatory (1987: 131, 133–4, 136). Burton's most public achievement was not to make everyone happy, but to provide amenities that were no less thoughtful than they were functional.

Art in the Park, Art as the Park

The cultivation of land for human enjoyment is millennia-old, as is the recognition of art's ability to frame nature, not just adorn it. By the latter twentieth century parks devoted to the display of art proliferated, one of the best-known being Storm King Art Center in Mountainville, New York, founded in 1960 by two businessmen. At Storm King (which hosts over 400 large outdoor sculptures), the land was reconfigured to suit the art (Dempsey 2006: 62), and "gargantuan welded steel works, initially intended for urban plazas, were put out to pasture much to their benefit" (Boswell 1991). This era also witnessed the popularization of land reclamation projects, which sought to rehabilitate spoiled nature through art. As artist Robert Morris observes, such projects were expected to "fulfill a kind of sanitation service" and "wipe away technological guilt" or "at the very least," produce "tidy, mugger-free" parks (1992: 259–60). But by co-opting the respective strategies of art park and reclaimed space, Christo and Jeanne-Claude, and Nancy Holt, were able to enliven their staid conventions.

Installation pieces have become common fixtures of public art, but rarely do they attain the notice and popular acclaim of those by husband-and-wife team Christo and Jeanne-Claude. With *The Gates*

(1979–2005, it took 26 years to gain approval), New York's beloved Central Park became a massive, temporary art park. For 16 days 7,503 individual gates, vinyl armatures hung with swags of "saffron"-hued cloth, meandered through 23 miles of park paths. The enormity of such undertakings requires Christo and Jeanne-Claude to navigate an expanded sphere of political officials, local citizens, and project workers. As a result their work "presses esthetic issues to their social context ... A position must be taken not just by art folk but by the immediate public ... (which) is not a consequence of the work but its primary motivation" (O'Doherty 1981: 337).

Despite the artists' relationship to Central Park as longtime New Yorkers, and their sensitivity to the site (inspired by Frederick Law Olmsted and Calvert Vaux's initial plans, which included functional gates to secure the park at night), Jeffrey Kastner found their work to be nostalgically decorative. He likens *The Gates* to "plop art ... whose hulking forms seemed parachuted into place," lamenting their "failure of imagination" both politically and aesthetically (2005). I would counter that while not the most nuanced of these artists' gestures, *The Gates* was aesthetically effective, enacting an arresting study of contrasts. Their rectilinear forms played against the park's undulating contours, while the tendency to take in the project as a sweeping mass was undercut by the strong visual presence of each individual gate. The fabric, undisturbed and opaque, looked quite different when aloft with the wind or shot through with light, and the neutral palette of a New York winter was punctuated by emphatic color. Christo and Jeanne-Claude reinvented an iconic space and then, by quickly returning it to its former state, enlarged its meaning to include the memory of their work.

The Gates was a populist triumph as public art, even if aesthetics are set aside. Many people did not like the look of *The Gates*, complaining that it was too sprawling, and the "saffron" fabric was more like the hue of a traffic cone. But what nearly everyone – the art world, city residents, tourists, and the mainstream media – agreed upon was that *The Gates* could not be ignored. Demanding our attention, the work was "a genuine cultural phenomenon, an uncanny hiatus in New York's life as usual," which succeeded in wooing not only sightseers but many citizens of the "most expertly blasé city in the world" (Kastner 2005). It is fair to ask whether

The Gates' magnitude as a cultural event is enough to render the work "great art," though as Marcel Duchamp pointed out there is more than some futility in such categorizations. But beyond the media frenzy and hordes of visitors, what I most remember is that *The Gates* resonated with an optimism missing from New York since the tragic day of September 11, 2001.

Working with a two-third-acre plot situated at the intersection of major thoroughfares, Nancy Holt created *Dark Star Park* (1979–84, restored 2002), in the Rosslyn neighborhood of Arlington, Virginia, across the river from Washington, DC. Though she was originally commissioned for a sculpture, the artist convinced the various sponsors (the NEA, Arlington County, and the Kaempfer Corporation, which was constructing the adjacent office building) that she was capable of designing the entire park (Lippard 1989: 212). Holt worked collaboratively with local landscape designers, urban planners, architects, contractors, and engineers, and engaged in nearly every step of the process. She persuaded Kaempfer to alter its building design to be better integrated with the park, and secured permission from the state to include a traffic island in her plan. Holt even moved to Arlington County during the project so she could regularly supervise its progress (Broude 1991: 79). It might seem ironic that an artist well known for her work in remote locations would be attracted to such a bustling place, but Holt's environmental sensitivity served her well here. A formerly neglected and inhospitable "no man's land" was transformed into a usable, inviting park, countering the blight of development with a combination of green space, seating, and sculptural elements.

At *Dark Star Park* a myriad of related components suggest cosmological tableaux: a tunnel gives access to the park; low retaining walls provide seating; serpentine paths echo nearby streets; and gunite spheres, some with holes chiseled through them, are reflected in shallow pools. Holt described the spheres as "stars that have fallen to the ground" (Holt qtd. in Marter 1989: 316), which eclipse each other's visibility as one moves around, through, or by the park. *Dark Star Park* takes its cues from Holt's "locators" of the early 1970s. Informed by her training as a photographer, the "locators" were pieces of pipe tunneled through naturally occurring forms like sand dunes, which defined specific views of water, land, and sky (Hall 1983: 29). In the Rosslyn neighborhood project, holes piercing the spheres and a pipe embedded into the landscaped berm frame vistas inward toward the artwork and outward on its surroundings. The larger portion of the park that abuts the office tower is actually more intimate, organic, human-scaled, and topographically variegated than photographs suggest. These often make the park look sterile, as if it descended upon its site rather than being nestled into its sloping nook. The spheres and metal poles set across the street on the traffic island are less effective; though they connect forms across space, they are isolated and less welcoming. The poles seem discordant with the rest of the design, and a tangle of electric boxes and traffic lights become unwitting participants in the piece. In an effort to merge "historical time" and the "cyclical time of the sun" (Broude 1991: 79), Holt marked the shadows cast by these spheres and poles permanently on the ground. These align with the actual shadows cast each year on August 1, 9:32 a.m., the exact moment in 1860 when the town's founder acquired the land. But without prior knowledge of this astronomical effect, or reading the explanatory plaque, visitors to the park would be hard pressed to make the connection.

Yet the efficacy of Holt's design is at least partly due to her willingness to create "situations" rather than provide "monolithic abstractions," producing work that "fuses with" rather than occupies its site. As Joan Marter describes it, "Holt involves the visitor in a total spatial experience ... as the viewer moves through the park, the work unfolds and discloses itself, and he or she experiences the nature of perception" (1989: 315–16). In fact, the artist was mindful of her audience throughout the process; she presented her previous work at public meetings and solicited area residents' input about "their desires for the site," before presenting her plan to local officials for approval. Holt's park is not merely a host for the art, but the art itself, even though it might not always be recognized as such. Families play there, the kids running without hesitation all over its contours, enjoying a park rather than reverently admiring art. I concur with John Beardsley – this is a worthwhile trade-off. Holt's "concessions to intellectual and psychological accessibility" are likely to inspire continued appreciation for a place that otherwise would have remained abandoned (Beardsley 1981b: 45).

---------------------------- **Art as the Agora** ----------------------------

In the ancient Greek agora, a public square and marketplace that fostered political conversation and social interactions, American society found a metaphor for democracy and a model for its commons. According to Jürgen Habermas, the spirit of the agora was inherited by the bourgeoisie of the seventeenth and eighteenth centuries, private individuals who debated public issues, allowing the merit of the arguments rather than the identities of their proponents to determine the outcome (1962). Of course, the participants in this discussion comprised a limited group, much more so than our public sphere of today. Alan McKee suggests that with the development of modern social organization the private and public spheres have evolved as "separate from the people who inhabited them – something that you could move into and out of" (2005: 35). For numerous critics the current situation is worrisome, marked by concerns that the commons is being "increasingly displaced by an exaggerated private domain." Although architect Peter Calthorpe acknowledges the commons' essential role as marketplace, he frets that commercial purposes have eclipsed social ones, particularly in the formation of community and identity (1993: 23). Likewise, Mark Dery fears the mall's food court, "themed-parked for mass consumption," will displace the public commons and quell its democratic functions (1999: 171, 179). But as W. J. T. Mitchell suggests, such bleak views are countered by one in which the globalization of culture and evolution of technology create solidarity or offer "new forms of public resistance to homogenization and domination" (1990: 2). Witness the rise of "culture jamming," which reinterprets popular media by making guerrilla-style modifications of it (Thompson and Sholette 2004: 13). Culture jamming has its foundations in grass-roots activism, but utilizes technology (especially the internet) as a means of wide dissemination. For example, groups such as HackThisSite and the Electro Hippies Collective practice "hacktivism"; employing computer hacking skills to undermine what they consider to be unfair or usurious corporate practices. The goal is "to change the way that people think about the world by playing with existing culture," in hopes of increasing political awareness if not necessarily inciting change (McKee 2005: 172–4).

Perhaps public art's noblest function is to nurture participatory citizenship, to create an unfettered intellectual space for debate and socio-political engagement that is not necessarily tied to a physical place. Phillips insists that public art can happen literally anywhere, and take any form; it provides a forum rather than occurs in one (1988: 93–4). She described this forum as the "mental landscape of American public life," which permits "dynamic, often conflicting expressions" and can even be "the space of dissent" (1992: 298). Although the commons can indeed assume many forms, its recent digital manifestations, which reinforce egalitarianism, are the focus here. Cyberspace extends social networks with the potential for knitting together individual lives from far-flung corners of the world in a single instant. The internet usurps not only geographic borders, but many socio-cultural ones as well (minus the important exception of economic barriers that preclude ownership of or access to a computer). As such it constitutes a domain for unregulated exchange in which intimately private moments are made available for public consumption. The private home has long been a site for public action, and can bridge the gap between these spheres. Sitting alone in a living room watching a popular television program, one still partakes in a shared social experience. When a person uses a computer, she acts individually, but participates in a collectively cultivated, community space: blogging, surfing websites, visiting chat rooms, or posting comments on discussion boards. Miriam Rosen described the internet as a "space which is not a place," though it invites personalization through our navigations and modifications of it. By the mid 1990s she insisted that "it no longer makes sense to speak of a viewer or even a spectator"; on the internet everyone is an active "user," charting her own itinerary (1996: 87, 95).

Artists who use the internet not just as a conduit for their art, but as a medium in its own right challenge the conventional art world, still resistant to change or unable to cope with the digital realm. *Listening Post* was created through collaboration between two "self-described computer geeks," and uses the ubiquity of everyday communications on the internet as its media. In 2000 artist Ben Rubin, and Mark Hansen, a professor of statistics, were brought together by Bell Labs to experiment with the relationship between art and technology, the end result of which was *Listening Post*. The *Post* is composed of 231 miniature LED screens hung on an 11 by 21-foot curved grid. Although programmed to seek common phrases, its searches also yield random ones, gleaned from the endless network of real-time exchanges at any given moment on the web. These phrases are converted into sound through voice synthesizers, while being simultaneously displayed on the screens. The effect is hypnotic: disembodied words and sounds become repeating patterns. Though *Listening Post* culls material from the internet's "public" spaces, it becomes "voyeuristic" when we realize these conversations were never intended for museum audiences. It seems fitting that the piece found a permanent home at the San José Museum of Art, in the heart of Silicon Valley (Clark 2006: 32–3), though its installation in a solitary gallery at the Whitney Museum of American Art was particularly evocative. But it is not siting that makes the *Post* public; it is its content and manner of construction. *Listening Post* covertly bucks elitist art world pretensions. Though the artists defined its theoretical and physical frameworks, having written the program and designed the mode of display, the continuously changing content is provided by unspecified internet users. What is happening in the news, their personal lives and private thoughts, or anything that compels them to comment on a bulletin board or in a chat room can become the art. Colette Gaiter asserts that the internet's most "public" art is that which permits viewers to contribute in its authorship (1995). In the case of *Listening Post* members of the public become collaborators, if unwitting ones. Without their (inter)activity the project could not exist.

The GALA Committee's *In the Name of the Place* (1995–8) offers another example of popular media's ability to create and disseminate public art. The committee was spearheaded in 1995 by artist Mel Chin, who was then teaching at the University of Georgia, Athens, and had also been invited for an artist-in-residency at the California Institute of the Arts, a progressive art school outside of Los Angeles. Chin was asked by the Museum of Contemporary Art (MoCA, also in LA) to participate in its upcoming exhibition, *Uncommon Sense* (1997), which examined the intersections of contemporary art and public interaction. This invitation spurred Chin to coordinate the efforts of faculty and students in Georgia and LA (hence the acronym GALA), and form a collaborative group which eventually included other artists and grew to 102 members. GALA adopted a slow, methodically "viral" approach to art placement, through which their works infiltrated "the organism of the television industry" (Dziewior 2000). According to Chin, "Eventually your host is the replicating agent" (Arning, Chin, Jacob, and Kwon 2006). *In the Name of the Place* used a highly popular TV series, *Melrose Place*, as its host. The show, produced by the Spelling Entertainment Group, was a campy, deliciously trashy primetime soap opera for which GALA produced some 150 site-specific props (Decter 1997). These addressed hot-button social issues ranging from safe sex to political protest, and made their way into 300 scenes over two seasons. For example there were the *Safety Sheets*, bed linens printed with a funky pattern that upon closer inspection revealed itself to be unrolled condoms. (Images of unrolled condoms were not allowed to be shown on TV; however, the offending design was so subtle as to escape the notice of the Federal Communications Commission.) *Fire Flies* was a painting reminiscent of Ross Bleckner's, but based on photographs of the bombing of Baghdad. Other props included a Chinese food take-out container, printed with slogans from the Tiananmen Square protest; and the *R U486 Quilt*, which bore the chemical structure for the "morning-after pill." Thus works of "high art" subversively entered the "low-brow" culture of television soaps, and together they forged a new public art.

At first GALA initiated these actions. After screening advance copies of upcoming episodes, group members would create different props without claiming individual authorship. Members of the *Melrose Place* cast and crew were often unaware of these first interventions. But over time, some of the show's set decorators, writers, and producers became GALA members, and began building plots around the objects. MoCA even became a location for one of the series' episodes, in which the careful observer can see Chin, an "extra" in the background. In the *Uncommon Sense* exhibition, GALA was represented not only by the props, but *Melrose Place* video clips and a set from the series, "Shooters Bar," which museum visitors could enter. In November 1998, the project culminated with the props being auctioned at Sotheby's, Beverly Hills; the proceeds from this high-rent event were donated to educational charities.

Despite the disdain of many academics, TV is a commonly shared public space in our culture, and a viable host for public art. Since GALA did not moralize about this medium, the group was able to utilize it to powerful effect. Instead of TV being the antithesis of art, as it is often and unfairly categorized, GALA made TV the subject, medium, and means of distribution for its "fine" art. Joshua Decter suggests that *In the Name of the Place* united two of conservatives' favorite "scapegoats," artists and the "popular but morally questionable TV show," to create a highly evocative "new type of cultural fusion" (1997). In a way elitism still persists here; one needs to be an art world insider who knows GALA's project, or a fan who has viewed enough *Melrose Place* reruns, to recognize and contextualize the artworks. But in another sense the project is quite egalitarian: anyone with a TV has the chance to uncover GALA's embedded socio-political subtexts, which challenges stereotypical notions of the TV viewer's passivity and limited intellect. A mainstream TV series, blamed for sensationalizing social issues to secure a young, hip audience, became the platform from which to treat such concerns seriously and disseminate them widely, even if the audience was unsuspecting or remained unaware. And with the worldwide syndication of the series, these issues may be explored across cultures and into perpetuity.

Art as Pilgrimage

The term "pilgrimage" is perhaps too oft-used to describe art outings; traveling far distances to see famous works or visit renowned museums. But the kind of pilgrimage I have in mind is more rigorous, requiring greater effort and commitment from the pilgrim. Walter De Maria's *Lightning Field* (1977; first opened to visitors in July 1978) fits the bill, transforming spectacle chasers into "pilgrims." Blogger Todd Gibson, acknowledging the "cloak and dagger" circumstances required to visit "De Maria's best known – but least seen – work," argues that these enhance the *Field*'s appeal and the status of those who make the trek. He uses the word "pilgrimage" thoughtfully "because *The Lightning Field* isn't just a piece you stop by to see on a lark" (2004a, 2004b). De Maria's idea for *Lightning Field* was influenced by his *Spike Beds* of the late 1960s; menacing grids of steel spikes, which required visitors to sign releases before entering the gallery (Smagula 1983: 291). In 1974 the artist built a small test field outside of Flagstaff, Arizona, while simultaneously conducting an exhaustive, multi-year search for the ultimate location – an unsullied, remote plot in the high desert of west central New Mexico, 7,200 feet above sea level. The *Lightning Field*'s "perfect arrangement" in a one-mile by one-kilometer grid is a "technological tour de force" (Adcock 1990: 45), employing sophisticated engineering and fabrication techniques. Its 400 stainless steel poles with their solid-pointed tips, each two inches in diameter, are set 220 feet apart (with an error factor of $\frac{1}{25}$ of an inch). Their varying heights (averaging 20 feet, 7 ½ inches) achieve uniform elevation despite the desert floor's irregularities. They slip elegantly into the ground (their concrete anchors are invisible), making a tangible connection between earth and sky, and marking a finite place amid what seems infinite space. De Maria's *Field* is an emphatic interjection into the landscape, but does not defile it. According to the artist, "the land is not the setting for the work but a part of the work" (De Maria qtd. in Smagula 1983: 290).

Lightning Field is a permanent installation commissioned by the nonprofit Dia Art Foundation, whose mission is to support "art projects whose nature and scale exceed the limits normally available within the traditional museum or gallery" (www.lightningfield.org 2006). The *Field*'s running and upkeep necessitates a full-time administrator who oversees archival needs, maintenance, and guest visits (Deitch 1983: 89). In traveling there the route becomes increasingly remote, and visitors must stay overnight (meals provided) at the on-site cabin. Albuquerque is the nearest city, about three hours away from Quemado (no public transportation is available between them), the tiny town where Dia maintains a humble office. There visitors – no more than six are permitted at the *Field* at one time – sign waivers releasing the foundation from responsibility in case accidents occur while visiting the work. A Dia representative then drives them on dirt roads about an hour north (43 miles) to the *Lightning Field*, where they are left for approximately 24 hours before someone picks them up. This Dia escort is quite necessary; in the absence of distinguishing landmarks or signage one would never find the place alone. The cabin has no televisions or computers, only a phone for emergencies (most cells cannot get reception). For city dwellers this kind of isolation is nearly inconceivable, and for some visitors might seem threatening. On the way there you likely think that the *Field* "better be worth all this effort"; when you get there you realize it is.

At first the level of control De Maria, and Dia on his behalf, exercises can be overwhelming. Your schedule, pocketbook, and connections to the outside world are all temporarily hijacked, which is a bit intimidating or infuriating, until you understand that the artist got nearly everything "right." The *Field* demands an extended, immersive visit to fully comprehend its nuances. By holding the visitors captive (so to speak) and purging all distractions, De Maria grabs and maintains our attention. A meditative tone and intense focus prevail; even when traveling as a group, people often opt – and are encouraged in Dia's literature – to make solitary explorations of the *Field*. Yet a feeling of camaraderie develops, even among former strangers, in sharing lodging, meals, and this unique experience. The cabin originally extant on the site was slightly expanded; simply appointed but cozy, it encourages quiet contemplation or thoughtful conversation. It is visible anywhere from the *Field*, a comforting presence in the midst of expansive wildness. Your time here is built around astronomical shifts of night and day, not hours on a clock.

The geometric purity of the *Field*'s grid and its spare aesthetic give rise to a sublimity befitting the Romantic tradition. Museums or even cities could not encompass the vast visions of earthwork artists, who rose to prominence in the 1970s. Their move outdoors marked a quest for a bigger swath of space, scale representative of the technological age, and direct relationships to the land. But it also intimated a desire to buck the economic and social structures inherent in cultural institutions, to enter into a "dialogue with the outside world and society at large" (Matzner 2001: 16). Reminiscent of prehistoric megalithic structures and eighteenth-century landscape spectacles, massive site-specific earthworks could not be conventionally bought and sold, owned and displayed. Such works possess an "archaeological quality" emphasizing the experiential, especially since they resist visual apprehension as holistic entities (Lippard 1967/68: 232). Viewing the *Field* in a single grand sweep is quite different than walking its uneven terrain. The perimeter (3.2 miles) is the most worn path, but helps one grasp the *Field*'s scope. Hiking straight lines through *Lightning Field* is more difficult; a diagonal route is harder still. Yet the *Field*'s interior offers surprises: elevation changes; a "lake" not visible in any of the photographs I have seen; and a rock cairn "shrine" marking the travels of devout pilgrims. The viewer's physical and psychological exploration here is primary; perceptual shifts constantly occur as one walks amid the shiny poles, illusive in the distance or against the bright sky, then coming into sharp focus as one approaches. Lawrence Alloway characterized this as "a kind of dematerialization, a dismissal of mass or legible spatial cues" (1976: 54). For some viewers this might produce anxiety, not being able to perceptually gauge the space or one's relationship within it (Baker 1976: 80). The tall, thin poles are majestic and yet vulnerable, set in a vast desert floor ringed by mountains. One is less struck by how large the *Field* is than how small it looks compared to its surroundings (Adcock 1990: 44). The site prompts transcendent experience, enhanced by one's amplified footsteps and breath, and theatrical plays of colored light on the poles and desert flora and fauna. All places change with light and time, but we are usually too busy to notice; *Lightning Field* demands rapt attention, heightening our appreciation for temporal shifts (Wortz 1980: 173). I visit on an unseasonably cold fall day; it both rains and snows in Quemado. A fog rolling over the *Field* gives way to a spectacular sunset and a frosty sunrise. At night, away from metropolitan light pollution, stars suggest an otherworldly observatory. Before I have left, I know I will come back.

Perhaps most people consider a lightning strike the work's consummation though only about 30 direct strikes might occur in a year (Adcock 1990: 46), mostly from late July through August. The piece provides opportunities for strikes without guaranteeing these; the grand majority of visitors leave without seeing *Lightning Field* "in action." Dia insists witnessing a strike is not the point;

"*The Lightning Field* does not depend upon the occurrence of lightning but responds to many more subtle conditions of its environment" (www.lightningfield.org 2006). Yet the foundation charges $100 more per a person for reservations in the stormy season (it currently costs $250 to visit then). Every viewer probably wishes for a lucky strike – a climatic moment putting weather on visual display. But *Lightning Field* is not about the lightning, really. It is about the agency of visitors, who remove themselves temporarily from daily life to commune with De Maria's work. In this sense, the *Field* is thoroughly populist in intent; it counters traditional museum culture, employs weather – a force that cannot be owned, and only occasionally, harnessed – as its medium, and relies upon viewer interaction. It firmly resists art history's celebration of timelessness, though it does not shrug off notions of preciousness (an art foundation lovingly cares for it in perpetuity). Unwilling to be physically or conceptually confined within a museum's envelope of climate-controlled zones and Plexiglas, *Lightning Field* exists in the here and now, waiting for weather's ephemeral effects to be visited upon it.

On one hand, *Lightning Field* is a privately sponsored real estate development project, spawning a steady flow of art tourism. But on the other, it is a pilgrimage site, requiring significant investments of time, money, and effort. The sense of specialness that punctuates *Lightning Field* is appropriate; it stages intense physical and psychological encounters of "long duration and slow use," quite "the opposite of brief or expendable" (Alloway 1976: 51). The purposefulness with which one visits the piece, the sustained focus it requires, and its isolation from everyday life affirm that *Lightning Field* is extraordinary and worthy of such devotion. (Even De Maria regularly visits.) Visitors cannot take photographs (though Dia sells slides), as both the *Field* and cabin are copyrighted. Photos could undermine the artist's contextualization or suggest that documentation substitutes for firsthand knowledge. De Maria banned photos of his earthworks in 1967, satisfied to have a few visitors experience them fully, rather than disseminating their images so that many people think they had (Smagula 1983: 289). But since the trek there is so arduous most people, even art world insiders, know *Lightning Field* through second-hand sources not direct experience (Baker 1976: 84).

Elizabeth Baker characterizes earthwork artists as a "curious mixture of self-removal and self-aggrandizement," whose secluded works seem "bizarre, even suspect." She suggests that *Lightning Field* could be perceived as "a very extreme form of artistic individualism, and its isolation in the desert as the apotheosis of the privileged setting – of the ultimate studio situation" (1976: 83–4). Likewise Morris contends that privately funded, distantly sited artworks are not really "public art" because there is limited physical access to these (1992: 251). On one hand, he is certainly correct. The *Field* permeates with an air of elitism; its far-flung site and pricy admission fee make it a destination for art world initiates, rather than a stop for curious travelers unable to stumble upon it on their own. But can we qualify a work's publicness by quantifying its audience? In response to this question one might compare *Lightning Field* to De Maria's *Earth Room* (first staged 1968, Munich; the current New York version was originally exhibited in 1977, reopening in 1980 as a permanent installation). *Earth Room* does not require that we go to the land, but brings it to us; filling a gallery (maintained again by Dia) with 280,000 pounds of dirt to a height of 22 inches, covering 3,600 square feet of prime real estate. It eradicates any other "impinging claim on the space" (Crow 1996: 141), and recalls SoHo's former life as an art hub (Dempsey 2006: 123). But while a SoHo gallery may be physically accessible to more people than the New Mexico desert, it is not necessarily any more public or comprehensible. And one cannot enter *Earth Room* as one can *Lightning Field*, its entrance being sealed with glass. At both sites the artist provides minimal logistical information so that visitors draw their own conclusions. De Maria asserts: "The sum of the facts does not constitute the work or determine its esthetics" (De Maria qtd. in Dempsey 2006: 107). At *Lightning Field* the viewer's agency is essential. Its 400 poles cannot constitute the artwork alone; without the location, climatic changes, and visitor's interaction, these would remain inert. There is more than a little irony in Dia, a foundation aiming to "make art experiences more widely available to the public" (Smagula 1983: 293) sponsoring such remotely sited work. But *Lightning Field*'s more rarefied aspects unearth (pun intended) its most public function: beyond satisfying a thirst for spectacle, the *Field* makes queries of larger

social relevance. As Morris noted, such works raise "moral questions …
as to where art should be, and who should own it, and how it
should be used" (1992: 256). Trekking through the "middle of
nowhere," scanning the ground for rattlesnakes while literally
waiting for lightning to strike, such questions become inevitable.

In most respects *Lightning Field* is anything but public: it is
removed from daily life, sited on private land, maintained by a prestigious foundation, autocratically controlled, and requires leisure
time and expendable income to visit it. It is a stop on art enthusiasts' Grand Tour, rather than a place known to the public at large.
Yet its conception feels decidedly public, much more so than the
plop art that lingers in city squares. Although the *Field*'s cachet is
derived from its exclusivity, its ability to foster highly personal reun-
ions with nature could certainly have broad appeal. Admittedly, the
"average" person will unlikely find her way here, pay the money,
and stay overnight for an art experience. But if one did, hopefully
she would feel welcome. As De Maria's assistants, Robert Fosdick
and Helen Winkler, remarked, "Everyone is the same at the *Lightning
Field*" (Fosdick and Winkler qtd. in Wortz 1980: 173). Despite
initial pretenses, the *Field* cuts through much art world posturing
to offer immediately visceral and sensory, yet deeply resonant and
introspective experiences relating to many people's lives. One sunset
at *Lightning Field* might be enough to convince even the biggest
skeptic that there is something meaningful and worthy in all of this
"art stuff."

Chapter 3   Culture to Go:
From Art World to
The World

*A museum can never be read as a single text. Even if we consider
the most basic question of who or what museums are for, there is
never a unitary answer. (Jordanova 1989: 32–3)*

Museums expose frictions between the public and the private. While
its roots reach back to ancient Egypt and Greece (the *mouseion*
being a sanctuary dedicated to the Muses), today's museum is most
closely descended from personal collections assembled in the last
several centuries. These are embodied in the Renaissance
Kunstkammer, literally an "art-cabinet" filled with aesthetic
treasures, collected by those with power and privilege in order to
demonstrate their mastery over and reach around the world (Duncan
1991: 93). By the end of the nineteenth century, Martha Ward
contends, the developing art market and consumer culture steered
art display, once "a civic form or public arena," toward more privatized realms (1996: 456). But less than a century later this situation
reversed itself with renewed focus on museums' public functions
(Hein 2000: 144). Art museums, the focus of this chapter, have
increasingly paid attention to issues of civic engagement, especially
in the last decade or two, creating vastly more hospitable environments for their visitors as compared to the past. But while com-
mendable, these efforts can nevertheless leave many potential
visitors estranged, finding the museum off-putting, intimidating,

or irrelevant. In 1938 Lewis Mumford observed that museums seem quite elitist; "half safety-deposit vault, half show-room," with the largest of these proffering "purposeless congestion and intellectual bewilderment" (1938: 446–7). This characterization is still true for some to this day. Although the museum now extends a much warmer welcome to the community at large, it remains the territory of the initiated; those with education, social status, and/or wealth make most of the decisions on its nature and function, often beyond the public eye. While public programming at art museums has certainly multiplied and demonstrates heightened sensitivity to all kinds of visitors, these initiatives continue to fall short of eradicating elitism. Despite their good intentions, museums need to better recognize and address such deficiencies. In over 15 years of teaching, there has never been a single semester in which most of my students said they conceived the museum as a place for them, one they seek out because they feel genuinely welcomed and appreciated there, and fully confident in their abilities to negotiate personal relationships with the art. Even in large urban centers where cultural resources are usually plentiful, for many students (especially at the entry level), art museums are the quintessential, unapproachable ivory towers, and it takes sustained consideration and multiple museum visits to convince them otherwise. This situation is neither completely of their making, nor is it unique.

Hilde Hein describes the art museum as a celebration of "the taste and refinement of those who would dictate the conditions of culture." She concludes "though now objectively available to all," museums "still maintain the value system of the privileged few" (2000: 20). Meanwhile tensions continue to mount regarding the museum's function, as institutions struggle to inform and even entertain audiences, while protecting and contextualizing their art (Edson and Dean 1994: 13). At American museums, frictions between the public and private become even more pronounced. In Europe, many museums are state-founded and -funded, "establishments of the body politic" like public schools or parks. But most American museums were built, established, and maintained by the private sector, and remain reliant on their founders' visions. Yet such privatization does not eclipse the "common good," as evidenced by venues such as the Museum of Fine Arts (MFA) in

Boston, incorporated in 1870 by a state legislative act but founded with private funds from both the general public and wealthy benefactors. The MFA was dedicated to the "elevated enjoyment of all" (Rathbone 1984: 39–42), an "oasis of order and culture" especially for the working masses (Levine 1988: 201–2). The American museum's private heritage and public mission intersect ironically: elite culture is preserved and made available to everyone (Wood 2004: 107–8). Clearly, the duality of the museum's public face and privileged nucleus shall continue to coexist.

The public's agency at the museum – much like populist intent in public art – is on the rise and garnering critical attention, particularly in the last 10 to 15 years. For Hein, late twentieth-century public art serves as a direct model upon which to recontextualize the museum. Though museums are now more consciously experiential and egalitarian, she notes many people still conceive them as "static structures," lofty seats of universal, eternal values. She urges museums to adapt the dynamism of public art to their own purposes; embracing temporality, pluralism, participatory practices, social activism, and experimentalism, while being more self-critical (2006). Like Hein, I advocate for public agency at museums, although my purpose here is not to reconstitute the museum along the lines of a contemporary public art paradigm. Instead I aim to examine the museum's publicness in broader terms, and more specifically as a potential site for public art. This chapter asks why the museum (and by extension the gallery) endures as the preeminent host for art, but remains under-utilized as a public art site. Is it merely a venue or an entrance fee that marks the distinctions between "art" and "public art"? If so, then how might the museum become part of public art's expanded terrain? If not, can we better articulate genuine differences between public spaces and private institutions, or should we even try to renegotiate those boundaries? While there are all kinds of art museums, with a variety of missions, collections, and populations to serve, for many people the "museum" concept exists as a holistic entity. It is also true that while museums cater to wider patronage than ever before, providing more interactive, immersive experiences for these visitors, they are still likely to impose institutional agendas upon them, albeit often well-intended ones. Therefore this chapter offers some suggestions about how museums might become even better listeners, more fully responsive to and deeply involved with audiences. To do so, museums must further transcend public conceptions of them as monolithic enterprises, and enhance their role as independent social and aesthetic forces within individual communities. Patricia Phillips contends public space is widely "communal," not the sole purview of local constituents; "psychological ownership" is not relegated to geography (1988: 94–5). On one hand, I most certainly agree. It is too easy a "solution" to say that community involvement surely begets a public art. But conversely, I shall emphasize the importance of community members being more directly engaged with their museums, especially by interacting more consistently and meaningfully with artists and museum staff.

At this juncture, a more expansive definition of "community" is necessary, which extends beyond geographical proximity to include shared values, traditions, or history that bind individuals into collective entities (Gee 1995: 62). We must also acknowledge the continual flux of "community," and the dangers of becoming too regionally bound in its definition. Community participation does not automatically produce a public sphere of action. But investments of time and effort from both museums and their users can create mutually beneficial bonds, which likely stimulate more inclusive forums for exchange. Such inclusiveness does not equal a least-common-denominator approach to art, or require consensus in decision-making processes. Instead it means that more people feel welcome to ponder all kinds of artworks, even difficult ones, in a multitude of venues, including museums.

Artist Robert Morris once remarked; "If there is such a thing as public art, what then is private art? ... the term public art has come to designate works not found in galleries or museums (which are public spaces), but frequently in association with public buildings, and funded with public monies" (1992: 250). By isolating issues of location and funding, Morris points up faulty logic in the abiding criteria by which art is deemed "public." If an artwork is placed where the public can come into physical contact with it without charge, then it is quickly categorized as "public." But this simple formula privileges physical over intellectual and emotional accessibility; instead of conceiving these as three interrelated, mutually dependent components, it reduces art experiences to commercial transactions, or the lack thereof. It also ignores an inherent irony

Morris underscores; museums are actually quite *public* places, and as Rosalyn Deutsche asserts, "socially constructed spaces" (1992: 159–60). It follows then that museums are rich potential sites – both physically and psychologically – for public art. Yet we continually segregate museums as discrete entities from other public sites; places like train stations and airports are perceived as more public than museums. In fact, the organization of and access to facilities in all of these is similar; at each, users enter a lobby-like space and move about with relative freedom, but to partake of services offered within – whether to utilize transportation or view art – we pay some sort of fee. Paradoxically, an openly "commercial" gallery is, in some ways, more thoroughly public. While it offers no pretense about its purpose to sell art, generally anyone is able, free of charge, to view its works. Although one may feel less welcome at or intellectually prepared for the gallery, it presents no inherent economic barriers to looking at art (buying is an entirely different situation). Likewise, despite museums' perceived exclusivity, they provide actual spaces and cerebral fodder for exploring art, personal values, social issues, and civic responsibility; essential ingredients in defining public life. A museum becomes most fully public when it prompts us to examine our aesthetic tastes, cultural beliefs, and social practices, and when a variety of visitors feel comfortable and properly equipped to actively partake in such investigations. To accomplish such lofty aims, museums and their respective publics must depend more upon one another, with both parties shaping institutional infrastructures and conceptual frameworks. If museums do not mold the public to their will but invite sustained participation in matters ranging from programming to operations, they can transform visitors into genuine partners with shared visions for the future. Powerful art experiences are not reserved for museum audiences (Senie 1989: 301), and conversely, public art is not relegated to city streets.

What Museums Do for Us

Art museums are places where good things happen; people get interested in art, have up-close encounters with it, and can ask questions and even find answers. But their common function is strangely incongruous; to provide "elite experience for everyone" (Hein 2000: 17–18). Many public institutions grew out of personal collections for limited audiences, and even government-sponsored ones likely rely on private revenue as well as public monies. Regardless, if a museum posits itself as a public trust preserving culture for future generations, and makes this culture available to broader audiences, it assumes a dimension of public responsibility. But tensions between a museum's private interests and public mission create palpable friction at times, and can even cast an institution as unfriendly in the eyes of those it supposedly serves. In very real ways, museums are fortresses. With proper conservation practices and security measures in place, they physically protect artworks that might otherwise perish. Within a museum, art is much less likely to be vandalized than on a city street, and can remain virtually unaffected by time and weather. Thus, a museum is a kind of life support system for many artworks, extending their existence into perpetuity. But museums can be perceived as intellectual fortresses as well, purviews of those initiated into the ways of the art world, with the background and education to understand the art housed inside.

Museums do not exist only to ensure their own futures and that of the art they safeguard; they aim to make art accessible and available to the public. Museums are also sites for civic pride. No city achieves "world-class" status without at least one truly impressive, usually encyclopedic, museum. But in small towns even regional museums are prized, bolstering the visibility and identity of a community. One does not have to personally visit a museum to benefit from its existence. To know it is there, as an enduring symbol of culture confirming a community's value, is often enough. Museums frequently resemble places of worship, and function like them as well. As Carol Duncan notes, "museum space is carefully marked off and culturally designated as special" (1991: 91–2). Since museums isolate art within their walls, they position themselves as pristine, distinctive spaces to have "art experiences," unlike urban settings with their cacophonies of "competing visual stimuli" (Senie 1992b: 230). No one goes to a museum and is surprised to find art there, in the way one may be caught off guard by a sculpture at a bus stop. Museums are purposeful places for art; people visit to have deliberate encounters with the works inside. Everything a museum enshrines is easily designated as "art." With the prestige, protection, and context of a museum comes the assertion that while one may not like its works, one cannot question that they are, indeed, art.

An extension of a museum's ability to confer status is found at the commercial gallery. Profit-making galleries play essential roles in the contextualization, promotion, and distribution of art, and their agendas frequently intersect with those of museums. Financial concerns are inextricably tied to art, even at a museum, which is ultimately "a (false) refuge from commodification" (Ward 1996: 452). These economic realities are not necessarily undesirable or unsavory, though in cases of corporate sponsorship motivating factors can be suspect. Over the last 30 or so years it has become increasingly necessary for museums to accept such sponsorship. For example, Philip Morris has engaged in decades of generous art patronage, but also made major financial contributions to Senator Jesse Helms, who led the charge against the National Endowment for the Arts (see Chapter 1; Dubin 1992: 260–1). Through art patronage the cigarette manufacturer wishes to transform its public image into that of the good citizen – socially consciously and phil-anthropic. In return for its money, Philip Morris receives the implicit endorsement of cultural institutions, the subtext of which pro-claims: "The museum says we're okay, so you should like us too." Hal Foster maintains that we should be rightfully wary of corpora-tions whose relationship to culture "is less one of noble obligation than that of overt manipulation – of art as a sign of power, prestige, publicity" (1985: 4). Mark Rectanus concurs, noting that such sponsorship can "deflect attention away from the corporation's own functions as a cultural producer, promoter, or mediator" (2002: 5). But Howard Smagula suggests that corporate "self-interests do not necessarily cast doubt on the sincerity" of commitment, though emphasis on public recognition often channels such funding toward blockbuster exhibitions (1983: 16–17). Museums face persistent challenges in balancing their complex networks of potential audiences, which include art enthusiasts, tourists, schoolchildren, community members, and various benefactors.

In assessing intentions behind the founding of museums, Charles Saumarez Smith contends they function to "remove artefacts from their current context of ownership and use, from their circulation in the world of private property, and insert them into a new environment which would provide them with a different meaning" (1989: 6–7). Virtually every artwork made prior to the late eighteenth century that now resides in a museum was never intended for that. Earlier art was destined for other public settings such as churches or city halls; created for ritual purposes rather than aesthetic ones; or designed for private display instead of public exhibition. Many of these works were conceived as *timely*, of-the-moment responses to particular historical moments or personal memories. Yet museums render art *timeless*, preserving it for all foreseeable posterity, regardless of its natural lifespan or original frames of reference. Certainly museums exist to educate us. But as Ludmilla Jordanova characterizes it, beyond its edifying functions a museum is a palace of wonders, eliciting awe at the proliferation, quality, and variety of objects shown (1989: 22). Museums woo and charm us, show us other sides of life, offer wonderment and surprise. As total environments, inclusive of their artworks, museums can be seductive spectacles. To be surrounded by beauty is a very powerful experience, and the attendant uplifting social and individual benefits to be reaped ought not be underestimated or discounted as frivolous. But while immersion in physical beauty may initially draw us to museums, the promises of intellectual and emotional discovery are likely to keep us coming back. As Dale McConathy insists, "The public doesn't need to be told that art is good for them but rather that it can be extremely enjoyable. The ultimate education should be exciting and pleasurable" (1987: 15).

Museums also function as arenas for critique. Here artists share work with colleagues, and garner critical responses from the art world and broader public. Visitors can have direct physical access to and gain much information about art; contemplating it in relationship to other works, and within the contextual frameworks museums provide (via wall text, installation, and so forth). Hopefully after careful consideration, viewers can determine whether or not to accept such frameworks and all of the assumptions that come along with them. This last step is the most difficult; confidence in our personal qualitative assessments can be shaken by museums. They are often large and even daunting places, where it is frequently – and usually correctly – assumed that the featured art must be good, as it was chosen by people who know about these things. Undoubtedly, educated museum professionals have a wealth of knowledge and experience, and museum-goers benefit enormously from their expertise. But specialized training does not cancel out the public's subjective critical faculties. Art invites opinions, and insightful ones come from all kinds of people, not just those with a particular pedigree or background. Clearly art museums are not the public's enemies, they are advocates. Yet "the museum" and "the public" have come to embody the perceived and actual struggles between elitist and popular culture (Rice 1992: 234–5).

The museum as a scholar's "temple for culture," coddled by modernist-era notions of exclusivity in which learned connoisseurs certified the genius of artists and the preciousness of their master-works, has its purpose. But as public institutions, museums must make art accessible and personally relevant to ever-broadening publics. Educational programs that "articulate and explicate" aesthetic criteria, rather than "establish or legislate" such would go a long way toward those ends (Senie 1992b: 227). Despite numerous, well-intended public relations overtures, which have expanded the sphere of museum audiences, many members of the public still feel intimidated by museums. Museums can effectively counter visitors' insecurities and doubts about whom they serve. When they do so, the public is far less likely to perceive them as depositories "for things that are dead" (Weil 1990: 87), or snobby establishments discounting the everyday experiences of "ordinary" people.

My Museum

In 1967 artist Allan Kaprow characterized museums as mausoleums for paying respect to the dead. Though he noted museums' "increasing concessions to the idea of art and life as being related," he maintained "they provide canned life" that is "like making love in a cemetery" (Kaprow and Smithson 1967: 59–60). Twenty years later, while participating in a public forum at New York's Dia Art Foundation, Douglas Crimp urged museums to pursue more programming outside of their spaces, and form "direct relationships to actual communities." Hal Foster replied to Crimp that this was a matter "not so much of sites as common ground" (Foster 1987: 47). Without an engaged, participatory visitorship personally invested in an institution's livelihood, a museum is a hollow endeavor. Although Chapter 5 provides a broader discussion of proactive roles played by the public, here it is essential to consider viewers' agency at museums. David Fleming suggests there exists "The Great Museum Conspiracy," evidenced by a lack of social inclusion and cultural equality. This "conspiracy" manifests itself through several interrelated conditions: who runs museums; the manner in which, and for whom they are run; and what museums contain. He concludes that even when publicly funded, museums have been "private and exclusive clubs" for an educated, prosperous minority. Thus despite their public service missions, museums have historically functioned as "agents of social exclusion, and not by accident but by design" (2002: 213).

At museums many of the decisions are already made for us. This is not necessarily a bad thing, as most choices were arrived at thoughtfully, by highly trained, well-meaning professionals. Yet this fact may account for why some people still feel unwelcome at museums, despite all the colorful banners and docent tours that beckon them. Museums ought not to be content to build "large audiences of passive, leisure-time consumers" (Joselit 1990: 145), or assume preexisting publics (Breitbart and Worden 1993: 28). As Elaine Heumann Gurian observes, museum professionals often want to be inclusive of varied populations, but can do a poor job of serving them; "we demand that they accommodate us and then wonder why they do not visit our galleries." She insists that her colleagues may, perhaps unwittingly, reinforce exclusive hierarchies of culture and knowledge. "If the audience ... feels alienated, unworthy, or out of place, I contend it is because we want them to feel that way" (1991: 176–7). Art professionals, especially museum directors, curators, and exhibition designers, must avoid any typecasting of the public as philistines, unable to digest what they see on their own. While the public can use guidance in understanding art, a museum is at its best a place to sharpen our critical faculties, not one where all of the analysis is done for us. Museum workers need to find additional ways to converse with visitors. Although many institutions reach out with surveys and various public programming, there could be more direct, candid conversations in which multiple publics explore their wants from a particular museum, and the individual institution examines whether it is feasible or desirable to pursue these goals. Such a process would be cumbersome for sure, but could stimulate additional usage of facilities and encourage deeper public investment in an institution, especially among community activists and those with strong personal interest in the arts, and increase comfort levels for all museum-goers. Many museums already offer "user-friendly" text panels, tours in which visitors chat with knowledgeable guides, and numerous lectures, events, and family days. Yet in most cases an institution rather than its users determines the dialogue's tone and depth (Spicer 1994). Museums can more regularly incorporate the opinions and ideas of their visitors, as witnessed by the Community Voices initiative at the Brooklyn Museum of Art, through which the museum solicits local residents' commentary to be included on text panels in the galleries. (Currently exhibitions of Egyptian, American, and European art utilize Community Voices text.) When patrons share in the intellectual and emotional ownership of a museum, they render it public.

Art history can seem like a monolithic field practiced by a homogenous group of people, deciding which artists deserve reverence and which artworks are worthy of preservation. Not only do museums offer protection within their walls, they also confer prestige. Once a work is included in a museum two assumptions are made: first, this thing is special and merits our attention and appreciation; second, art omitted from the museum is less interesting or important. It is not only a matter of which works are chosen for display, but the manner and context in which these are presented. For nearly every object that wins a place in a museum, an exhaustive installation process unfolds. Where and how should the art be placed? Which setting will best complement it? And what text is needed to *explain* it? This scenario carries problematic implications for public art; if the "good stuff" is found in museums, what value does art in other places and contexts hold? Is this, quite simply, not as good, or not good enough for a museum? Assuredly, museums are not the only sites at which to have meaningful, challenging encounters with art. But does their aristocratic history and authoritative nature preclude the ability to amiably host public art? Would populist initiatives beget more democratically run museums, or are public art and museums relegated to roles as more distant, even if admiring, cousins?

As places set aside for art experiences, museums are hopefully not antagonistic, though can never be fully neutral toward art. Even the supposedly blank, hermetic "white cube" still conveys modernist conventions of taste and value (Buren 1975: 316; O'Doherty 1976; 1981: 321–2). Of course many visitors come not just to see art, but the museums themselves; institutions that are famous, in lovely locations, artfully designed, or that utilize clever display tactics can overshadow the works they allegedly serve. For example, Frank O. Gehry's *Guggenheim Museum* (1997) in Bilbao, Spain, revived the former industrial city's economy. But the building's dramatic sculptural presence and idiosyncratic spaces seem to compete with many of its artworks. Even when the architecture and reputation of an institution do not overwhelm the art, the museum context never fades entirely. Visitors' experiences are negotiated through the behest of such institutions, which are unlikely to fully integrate art-works into their confines as happens more frequently in other public venues (see Chapter 2, *Art as Amenity*). At museums context is literally everything, and their presentation techniques often convey a "don't touch" mentality. From the practical necessity of restrict-ing physical contact with the art viewers might glean secondary messages: "This isn't really for you anyway – not for you to touch, not for you to understand." As Craig Owens posits, "while the museum claims to protect works of art in the name of the public, it actually protects them *from* the public" (1987: 19). Martha Rosler identified an "imperialist mind-set" at work here, meant to impress audiences with the "apparent control of time, space and precious resources – an awe of simple accumulation, like Scrooge McDuck in the money vaults" (1987: 12). Though museums were "aggressively designed to transform people into citizens by infusing them with a sense of cultural identity and shared patrimony," they still stratify social status. Hein contends museums offer "vicarious ownership" through limited access to precious objects, which shifts "attention away from the material inequity," glorifies "the displacement of wealth into a symbolic public sphere," and "softens the reality of exclusion by creating an illusion of shared history and aspiration" (2000: 21–2). In other words, a museum "paradoxically intensifies both access and exclusion" (Greenblatt 1991: 52).

Many assumptions about privilege in the museum world remain true. While demographics for museum-goers have certainly expanded over the last several decades, museum professionals are still highly educated (rightfully so), while museum benefactors and trustees are usually art collectors themselves, armed with financial resources, social clout, and educational opportunities far beyond most people's means. Although the doors of an art museum may be open to virtually everyone, symbolically it still sifts out the "haves" from the "have-nots" by connoting social class in various ways. Some of these are more obvious; expensive membership costs, exclusive VIP events, galleries or entire wings named after those making staggering donations. But more subtle caste distinctions also crop up: How familiar is one with art history prior to coming to the museum? How accessible or jargon-laden are the explanatory texts, pamphlets, and exhibition catalogues? How welcome does one feel amid an array of necessary but intimidating security guards and devices, which imply visitors cannot be trusted to behave appropriately here? Having money does not directly translate into a higher level of comfort at and appreciation for museums, but historically it has been an indicator for the likelihood that one will become an art admirer or collector, and a museum enthusiast. Members of the wider public need be genuinely convinced that museums care about what they, not just experts and the elite, think.

Some museums do a superb job of balancing personal agendas and public missions. The Isabella Stewart Gardner Museum in Boston is such a place. Conceived by its famously quirky and wealthy namesake, the Gardner Museum unapologetically presents a collection representing the tastes of a single individual. Every work is there because Isabella liked it, and displayed in a very particular manner conceived by her. This is unconventional given current museum practices; there is minimal labeling or explanatory texts within this purposefully de-institutionalized context of affluent domesticity. The Gardner is a visual hodge-podge, where unlikely juxtapositions come together; a swath of green evening dress hangs beneath Titian's *Rape of Europa*, as Isabella thought they complimented each other nicely! And strange circumstances ensue: frames remain hanging, notably emptied of their works after a theft over 15 years ago (no display can be drastically changed due to a highly restrictive founding charter). But the Gardner is refreshing in its blatant presentation of a lifestyle we can try on but most could never afford, and in Isabella's palpable enthusiasm for the art. This is in marked contrast to the exhibition, "Things I Love: The Many Collections of William I. Koch," which was hosted by the MFA, also in Boston (2005). Here the collection of a wealthy collector and major museum benefactor was put on display. Apparently Koch loves female nudes painted by modernist heroes, models of boats, large bottles of good wine, and firearms, as these were prominently displayed. What was so noteworthy about this exhibition was the museum's willingness to enfold Koch's vision into its own.

The Gardner Museum represents Isabella's viewpoint first and foremost, though she always intended to make her collections available to the public. At the MFA, guns in the galleries and yachts on the front lawn were out of place, not because these were too common to stand on the institution's rarefied ground, but because this particular museum seemed to have compromised itself. The MFA is not steered by a singular voice but operates under a collective body of art experts, functioning as an often unspecified but nonetheless authoritative guiding force. By showing Koch's collection, the MFA implicitly endorsed his tastes and agenda. The title of the exhibition is curious. "Things I Love" is ironically approachable, devoid of posturing jargon; Koch is everyman, just like the rest of us, except he races yachts and can afford to indulge nearly any whim. It is also as if the MFA tried to distance itself through the title: "Koch may love these things, but we're not so sure ..." An exhibition of this kind leads one to wonder about the museum's motives; was Koch's point of view really so enlightening it needed to be recognized and celebrated, or might the MFA have had other reasons for mounting the show?

Ultimately museums can frame but never control art experiences. They offer guidance and help determine what is important or of high quality, but cannot fix meaning or context. As Ward argues, we cannot "assume a normative viewer" who responds only to a museum's programmatic cues; there will always be those who "maintain their own ways of seeing" (1996: 461). Each visitor negotiates a personal relationship with the art and its institution. Each brings his own likes and dislikes with him to a museum, which directly impact the first impressions, considered opinions, and ponderous thoughts he will have while there. A museum can install an eighteenth-century period room with immaculate detail, attempting to make past symbols of wealth and leisure come to life for today's viewer. While one visitor may perceive the social underpinnings of such luxury, another may find the "implicit" sense of power neutered by the genteel pastels and dainty proportions favored in the Rococo age. As Spencer Crew and James Sims assess the situation, "a narrative is being constructed by the audience, whether the exhibition developers like it or not" (1991: 173). Throughout their evolution museums have been morphing, responding to contemporary tastes and social conventions, and changes within art history and museum practice. Out of necessity, and genuine desire too, they have become more inclusive places. Yet museums enact tensions not only between notions of the "public" and "private," but between the "communal" and "personal" too. A fully public museum entertains issues of collective consequence, makes overtures to mass culture without pandering to it, and nurtures individual viewers' confidence in their own critical abilities, social worth, and aesthetic tastes. These outcomes require good measures of mutual trust; audiences must believe museums have a multitude of their best interests at heart, and institutions need to have faith that visitors can discover art's meaning and relevance on personal terms. Making art accessible requires more than physical exposure. The types of education, outreach, and programming experiences museums provide can foster more vibrant, participatory interactions with a broader spectrum of visitors.

Education, Outreach, Programming

It is not surprising that many Americans relate to art as a strange, unwelcome, or hostile creature. In our country, art programs are often the first in line when school budget cuts loom, implying that art and its attendant bodies of knowledge are the most expendable components in a child's education. This attitude surely contributes to the ease with which people may disregard the insights of art professionals, emboldened by notions that art is an inherently subjective field focused largely on "luxury goods." While unlikely to discount the expert findings of scientists, some individuals are predisposed to quickly dismiss the high-minded opinions of "artsy" people who work in places like museums. There is a lot to be learned from a statement such as: "I don't care if *they* say it's supposed to be good – I know what *I* like." First there is the assumption that art is open to everyone's interpretation, as I contend it ought to be. But second, a prominent wedge is cleaved between museums and the public in which an "us versus them" mentality presides. If museums persist in using dialects of specialized knowledge only discernible to ears of the initiated, those who cannot understand are soon disenfranchised, feeling detached and even resentful. As museum professional Danielle Rice notes, many cultural institutions were begotten during the eighteenth century in the Age of Enlightenment, which purported art as a sort of "universal language" available to all. But this universalist approach can be inverted upon itself, whenever one's comfort level is challenged (1992: 233–4): museums are rejected as self-appointed loci of authority; art professionals' skills are downgraded; and difficult or unfamiliar artworks are unconsidered, lampooned, or forgotten. While museums may impress us and elevate art's stature, they are also targets upon which exasperated members of the public visit their frustrations. John Cotton Dana, a shaper of American museum culture and educational programming in the early twentieth century, worried that museums can be "awesome to a few, tiresome to many, and helpful to almost none" (Dana qtd. in Weil 1990: 53).

Despite their "standing as neutral" seats of expertise (Falk and Dierking 2000: 232), museums are hardly objective places. They always reflect the "values, attitudes and assumptions" of those who determine their physical and contextual manifestations (Weil 1990: 60). Although educational levels and urbane lifestyles cannot guarantee an understanding of art (Lippard 1967/68: 228), historically connoisseurship reigned over art history. Pierre Bourdieu posits

ough our relationships to art we accumulate "cultural
tatus tied to demonstrable knowledge of and appreciation
ular types of culture such as "fine" art (1984). Connoisseurship, the notion that expertise and rarefied experience should
be privileged in art's assessment, is problematic. At the worst it dis-
misses the public as homogenous philistines. This view is particularly troubling at the art museum, which supposedly exists to serve
and educate its visitors, not proffer "public tests of spectatorial
competency" (Ward 1996: 462). Stephen Weil suggested that a
museum's primary relationship to cultivate is with its audience, not
its collection, underscoring the social utility of providing stimula-
tion and public empowerment. By loosening its grip on the "authoritative or exclusive source of historical interpretation or aesthetic
judgment" a museum could "enlist the visitor as a collaborator who
might, in turn, develop his own sense of heritage, causality, con-
nectedness, and taste" (1990: 47–8, 53, 55–6). The opinions of
any visitor can be welcomed at museums. But while all judgments
are appreciated, should they be equal, all of the time? How can the
mediation of experts make "fine art" accessible to more people,
without oppressing viewers' own critical faculties? Can we really
integrate the ideas of laypeople into the daily operations of a
museum without that institution losing its authority? And finally,
how might we arrive at more nuanced assessments of cultural experience, rather than a barometer that only reads "high" and "low"
with few nodal points in between? The answers to such questions
are likely be found through establishing additional, clearer lines of
communication between the art world and the general populace,
heightening the number and type of cooperative efforts between
museums and their visitors.

Since the late 1960s, when museums emphasized their "public
service" and pedagogical functions while diversifying their audiences (Hein 2000: 143–4), visitorship has grown exponentially.
Museums have also often become sole providers of arts education.
It may be unfair to lay the bulk of this responsibility at the museum's
door, but given the "totally deficient" state of such education
in our public school systems there may be little alternative
(Senie 1992b: 224). In light of this recognition, museums would
be wise to conceive their visitors as characterized by Gurian: "partners"

in the museum experience, not inconveniences or passive receptors, but "inherently smart" and "entitled to ask questions and receive answers" (1991: 185). For her, fairness is at the heart of museum practice. Thus she maintains that visitors be encouraged to use museums "within their own personal frameworks," and museum workers to "overtly reveal their personal identities, backgrounds and points of view" rather than shielding these behind anonymous authority. Anything less, Gurian claims, would only uphold "the right of a nonelected power elite to transmit its values untested and unexamined" (1990: 12–13). Weil concurs the museum is no "transparent medium – a clear, clean, and undistorting lens" through which we have encounters with "pure and fresh" objects. Neither is museum-going "a tidy nor a predictable activity." He decries the hubris of a museum purporting methods of "one-way communication in which the facts, values, and skills possessed by those responsible for its operation are consistently superior to the facts, values, and skills possessed by its visitors" (1990: 47–8, 63). Likewise Charles Saumarez Smith insists the museum ideal of a "safe and neutral environment" that fixes interpretation is a false construction, as evidenced by museum objects that "retain vestiges" of their former lives in, "and passage through, the outside world." He concludes "a populist display need not be, in fact, should not be, patronizing in its conception of audience response," but must acknowledge the "multiplicity of different attitudes and expecta-tions and experiences" (1989: 9, 11–12, 19). In this way the cul-tural imperialism of museums is exposed and challenged. As Ivan Karp puts it, they "become sites where one not only asserts things but where there is also the possibility of questioning those very assumptions" (Karp and Wilson 1993: 267).

In the 1970s the United States witnessed the rise of artist-run galleries as alternatives to museums, with artists providing frames of reference for art as well as the art itself. Since then artist-run work-shops have become increasingly popular and present opportunities for museums to deeply engage their publics. In addition to the requisite artist's talk that is usually a fairly formal lecture, artists spending more time (perhaps in residencies) at institutions can have sustained, direct interactions with museum-goers. Artists could lead museum tours for patrons, underscoring their personal perspectives on an institution, and community members could bring visiting artists to their neighborhoods, increasing recognition of regional culture. Such interpersonal relationships would cement bonds not only between the individuals, but between the public at large and their museum. Museums could also enhance their function as conduits for visitors' agency; developing programs in which self-selected museum-goers help determine the frequency, type, and quality of art experiences at an institution, and within their own communities. Maybe the public could even be invited to weigh in on collections-management decisions or future building campaigns, without usurping the experience and wisdom of a museum's trained staff. In this way museums would retain "the expertise of the professional" but be enriched by "the cognition or expertise of non-professionals" (Miles 2004: 150). In other words, public voices would be featured more prominently in museums' choruses.

While these suggestions may sound naively idealistic, a variety of similarly minded initiatives have already occurred. For example, the Dia Art Foundation hosted *If You Lived Here*, a series of events addressing community, housing, and urban planning, conceived and directed by artist Martha Rosler (1987–8). "Town Meetings" were organized in conjunction with the events to encourage a more widely constituted public forum in which artists, community members, museum professionals, and interested parties could engage in spirited, frank discussions (Rosler 1991). At the Center for African Art in New York the exhibition, *Perspectives: Angles on African Art* (1987–8), investigated multivalent readings of African art. Ten individuals were invited to act as co-curators, choosing objects and discussing their particular viewpoints. Admittedly these were not laypeople but the diversity of the group, which included art historians, artists, an anthropologist, a writer, an archaeologist, and a banker who collected art, produced a richly textured dialogue as evidenced in the text panels. Instead of a "godlike voice of authority behind the selection of objects" (Gurian 1991: 187), the labels here provided "highly personal, arguable opinions" and designated the respective speakers. Thus the exhibition voiced multiple views, contested the definitive authority of museums (while still allowing the Center to be a disseminator of information), and underscored the complexity of cultural representations. *Perspectives* heightened visitors' awareness of the museum's subjectivity, not to make apologies for such, but as Susan Vogel asserts, to acknowledge that art "does not speak for itself" and is "filtered through the tastes, interests, politics, and state of knowledge of particular presenters at a particular moment in time" (1991: 193–5, 201). More recently, *The Interventionists: Art in the Social Sphere* (2004–5), an exhibition organized by the Massachusetts Museum of Contemporary Art (Mass MoCA), focused on the art of social engagement and protest as practiced by artist-activists working on the streets or with communities. Mass MoCA confessed it was not easy to showcase such art in a museum setting, which by necessity was often represented through reconstructions and documentary evidence. But the museum accepted that not all of the work could be hosted within its walls and was content to let some art spill out into the streets, having no physical presence in its galleries. Artists such as Haha and Krzysztof Wodiczko (see Chapters 5 and 6 respectively), not only represented but physically intervened in the socio-political sphere, directly engaging an "audience outside the insular art world's doors." Thus a "do-it-yourself" approach prevailed, emphasizing outcomes "beyond aesthetic pleasure" as artists embraced "outsider" roles to bond more closely with members of the public (Thompson and Sholette 2004: 13–14, 17–18, 21).

Clearly, facilities alone do not render an institution public. Comprehensive under-girdings of programming and outreach are essential if museums wish to enlarge audiences and enrich the depth of public connections. The new Institute of Contemporary Art (ICA) in Boston, opened in late 2006, kept its cutting edge intact while expanding its public mission. The 70-year-old institution is consciously positioning itself to be a cultural hub and community center, despite its more remote location in South Boston. (The ICA moved from a downtown location in a former police station to a waterfront site it received free from the city.) Although not bankrolled by "old money" like other Boston museums, the ICA is now building a permanent collection, a change spurred by larger facilities and the desire to raise its profile. These days many institutions are mindfully welcoming of the public; the ICA provides amenities that are commonplace in today's museum world (signed interpretation for events, large-print textual materials, audio tours to download on

MP3 players). But the Institute is using more than amenities and the spectacular new building by Diller Scofidio + Renfro to lure visitors. Though corporate patronage has firmly descended upon the ICA, this often supports populist-spirited initiatives that are quickly becoming trademarks of the reborn Institute (Bank of America presents the Art Lab, and Free Thursday Nights are sponsored by Target). Among its first exhibitions in the new building was a show featuring local artists competing for the James and Audrey Foster Artist Prize (formerly the ICA Artist Prize), which invited members of the public to vote for their favorites (the winner was decided by a peer jury). The Institute also boasts extensive programming and offers a selection of activities and events such as family days, classes, screenings, and musical and dance performances, some of which are free. The Art Lab is a hands-on studio for kids, and monthly Play Dates are sponsored in part by the NEA. The ICA's state-of-the-art media and educational facilities are regularly available to the public. Any visitor can use the breathtaking Mediatheque jutting out above the water, where computer stations provide access to the museum's video archive and other arts-based information. The Digital Studio is geared toward teens (public schoolchildren can receive scholarships), with courses in web design, animation, sound art, and photography. The Fast Forward after-school program allows teens to produce their own videos in consultation with professional filmmakers, and adolescents organize Teen Nights for their peers.

The ICA also hosts Vita Brevis, a public art program that came to the Institute along with its newly appointed director, Jill Medvedow, in 1998 (the program was independently established in 1997). Vita Brevis is significant because it directly acknowledges the role museums can play in public art, and formalizes the ICA's commitment to sponsoring it. Taking its name from the Latin phrase, "Ars Longa, Vita Brevis" (art is long, life is brief), the program seeks "unusual places" in Boston for temporary public artworks, including roadways, abandoned buildings, parks, and historic sites. It intends to build art audiences "outside of the mainstream museum" through collaborations with "non-arts organizations" such as neighborhood groups and churches. Vita Brevis aims to make contemporary art more vital in Boston, a city mired in its traditionalism, by seizing upon citizens' affection for and knowledge about local history and landscape (Medvedow 2004). Renowned – though perhaps unknown to the general public – artists have participated in the program, including Krzysztof Wodiczko, Cornelia Parker, and Jim Hodges. Each year Vita Brevis centers on a unifying theme or site to which an individual or group of artists responds. For example, *Art on the Emerald Necklace* (2000) consisted of eight temporary projects ranging from sculpture to performance, which took their cues from Frederick Law Olmsted's desire to promote socialization and democracy through public parks. Vita Brevis' latest installment, *Art on the Harbor Islands,* occurred in summer 2007.

Albert Elsen observed that public art is nearly always at risk – of rejection, disinterest, and neglect – but education can reduce its peril (1989b: 295). Museums can provide "preventative care" with programs that address and work through potential problems with the public. Effective arts education combines formal components like a lecture series, with less structured experiences such as self-guided tours around art venues. With increased awareness of and education about art, audiences are better equipped to make informed choices that widen museums' perspectives and expand their bases of knowledge. In short, instead of mostly imparting information to communities, museums could regularly call upon their visitors for insight and wisdom (Gee 1995: 62). In such a situation, visitors would probably be more tolerant of a variety of artwork, including that tackling provocative social issues or outside of their individual tastes. Understanding art's context does not guarantee its acceptance, but as Harriet Senie asserts, "an informed audience is usually a more open minded one" (1992b: 228). Visitors would also likely become more optimistic about their relationships to a museum, feeling they have direct stakes in its operation. Hein urges today's museums to foster their visitors' analytical skills: providing for conscientious "discrimination and discernment," which leads to "a culturally specific sense of intellectual, moral, and aesthetic values" and "self scrutiny and self-knowledge" (2000: 145–6, 148). A museum's educational value is at its height, and is most populist, when it acts as such a crucible, developing individual visitors' critical faculties. A museum that can excite people about art and encourage them to take initiative and action is a genuinely public one.

The Alternative Museum/
Alternatives to Museums

Historically, art museums have been keepers of convention; upholding established aesthetic principles, underscoring chronological evolution, and rendering the past as precious. Museums attest to individual artists' genius, emphasize the monetary worth of artistic endeavor, and reinforce conventional views regarding the scope, nature, and function of art. By the 1970s, many artists tired of these constraints and sought venues beyond the museum and commercial gallery, co-opting other-than-art spaces, and establishing cooperative and nonprofit alternatives. CoLab (Collaborative Projects) adopted a "parasite" approach to commandeer unused spaces, "sometimes extralegally." (CoLab's *The Times Square Show* was held in a former massage parlor and bus depot.) Another New York-based collective, Group Material, used storefronts and solicited its neighboring community's direct participation in exhibitions. Lucy Lippard describes such methods as "abrasively populist," allowing "the rough edges of the social stuff to grate against the smooth edges of the art stuff" (1989: 215–17). These artists did not so much overthrow museum authority, as reaffirm its health by questioning its precepts, limitations, and assumptions. By doing so, they helped delineate the museum's role, and conversely, identified the needs better served elsewhere.

In assessing the NEA's Art-in-Public-Places program (see Chapter 1), John Beardsley observed that art in a museum exists within a "protected context," bolstered by "professional opinion" and considered by viewers "predisposed … and receptive to it." He made a sharp distinction between museums and "public places" for a "more general audience," claiming that artworks encountered in the latter context, freed from a museum's "inhibiting authority," were open to greater public scrutiny and debate (1981a: 9; 1981b: 43). Andrew McClellan concurs that audience interactions with public art tend to be more "imaginative" that those within museums: "For better or worse, public art objects lead a more active life – a life of greater risk (of invisibility, disdain, and vandalism) but also of more varied engagement by a larger cross-section of people"

(2003: xiii–xiv). Clearly, we respond as much to the site at which art is experienced, as well as the attendant audiences and activities found there, as to the art itself (Senie 2003: 186–8). Though museums are actually much broader minded than their elitist reputations, they generally remain underutilized in terms of public art. One way to reverse this situation is for museums to invite artists and the public to interrogate their nature, function, and collections. Thus instead of isolating containers or decorative foils for art, museums serve as dialectical sites to investigate and even contest their own aesthetic and cultural heritages. As a museum loosens its clasp on definitive accounts of history it becomes a more pliable psychological and intellectual place, making "the social organization and ideological operations of that space visible" (Deutsche 1992: 166). For example in January 1969, curator Jan van der Marck asked Christo and Jeanne-Claude to do an installation at the new Museum of Contemporary Art in Chicago. They decided upon what would become one of their trademark gestures, and wrapped the exterior and interior (including draping the floors and stairs) of the museum. In *Wrap In, Wrap Out* the museum became the "subject for examination … the container, is itself contained." According to Brian O'Doherty, packaging the "museum (explicit) and staff (implicit) proposes that containment is synonymous with understanding" (1981: 334, 336, 338). As people sat on the floor, contemplating bare walls, their expectations of the museum as a host for art, and what that art is supposed to look like, were challenged. The museum, both concealed and revealed by the wrapping, actually became the art.

Eilean Hooper-Greenhill argues that in addition to information about objects on display, museum visitors also need to understand the history, layout, and collecting priorities of an institution itself, otherwise "the visit begins in a vacuum and it becomes hard work to make sense of subsequent experiences" (1994: 91). Artist Fred Wilson scrutinizes how museums frame spectators' gazes and expectations through selective representations of history, culture, and identity. As "an artist … African American and Native American … actually working in the museum at that time," Wilson "was in a position to notice some of the incongruities of these spaces." In 1992–3 he used a museum as his "palette," and created *Mining*

71

the Museum at Baltimore's conservative Maryland Historical Society. The artist was in concentrated residency there for a month and a half, and after that returned throughout a year. Wilson found it to be an "alien environment," but "realized it wasn't so much the objects as the way the things were placed that really offended" him. Through an exhaustive process, which included speaking to literally everyone who worked at the Society and looking at every object in its collection, Wilson was able to "mine" (to "dig" or "blow up" or to make it his own) the museum. The artist had a full floor of the museum and unrestrained autonomy, which he used to make interventions creating "a new public persona" for (and shedding some unflattering light upon) the Society. Wilson conceptually shifted objects already on view, and displayed many others that usually languished in storage, observing, "what they put on view says a lot about the museum, but what they don't put on view says even more." In one display he turned the backs of "cigar-store Indians" toward viewers "so that you couldn't look in their faces and accept the stereotype." On the wall behind these were photos of contemporary, local Native Americans, which the artist found outside the museum's collection after being told, "There are no Indians in Maryland." For another part of the exhibition, Wilson placed slave shackles in the same vitrine as ornate silverwork, so that the "beautiful" would be forced to acknowledge and coexist with the "horrific." Though Wilson's role in *Mining* is often perceived as that of a curator, he maintains that he acted as an artist, exploring how museum display shapes our views of the world and each other (Karp and Wilson 1993: 251–6, 258). Rather than "repressing the social conflicts" that constituted the museum's "very conditions" (Deutsche 1996: xviii), Wilson aptly exposed these, allowing visitors to draw their own conclusions.

Podcasts are another effective means of intervening in museum frameworks. In 2004 Art Mobs, an artists' collaborative comprised of students at Marymount Manhattan College under the direction of David Gilbert, a professor of Organizational Communication, began providing unofficial audio tours of the collection at New York's Museum of Modern Art (MoMA). Art Mobs' audio guides offer lively alternatives to the official recorded tour, a standard feature in many museums in which an expert, often a director or curator, takes visitors on an audio tour of a particular museum or exhibition. Although these official tours have evolved greatly since their inception (allowing visitors to choose the works they wish to hear about while bypassing others), they are still fairly linear and decidedly authoritative affairs. There are always those works they do not discuss, particular viewpoints they do not represent, or curious questions they cannot answer. While making the museum a more hospitable, user-friendly place for many people, these audio tours still reinforce a stratified hierarchy in which the legacy of art history and clout of the museum reign. Podcasts by people other than museum professionals cleverly intervene at particular physical sites, while interrogating the conceptual paradigms of all such institutions. Art Mobs' podcasts can be quite informational, but are more "entertaining," "playful," and "opinionated" than the standard audio tour ever dares to be, mixing casual observations, expert commentary, and music. In one podcast, student Cheryl Stoever and professor Jason Rosenfeld discuss Picasso's watershed work, *Les Demoiselles d'Avignon* (1907), chatting about the dawn of Cubism, the painting's evolution, and syphilis. Though the tone is irreverent, it is also loving: Art Mobs extends an apologia to MoMA on its website, proclaiming that they "hack a platform out of respect for it, because its elegance invites participation." The group seizes upon digital culture's inherent democracy (see Chapter 2, *Art as the Agora*), which erodes institutions' proprietary controls over their images and content. Art Mobs capitalizes on the ubiquity of MP3 players and ease of podcasting, imploring those outside the group to "Help us hack the gallery experience, help us remix MoMA!" (art_mobs 2004). The group offers to host other "homemade" MoMA audio guides on its own feed. Taking up the notion of "Remix Culture," Art Mobs prompts us to become more proactive consumers of media – museums included – and encourages museum-goers to experience the artworks for their own merits as well. Gilbert conceives the Art Mobs guides as personalized "soundtracks" through which to "sample" the museum: "We are democratizing the experience of touring an art museum; we are offering a way for anyone to 'curate' their own little corner of MoMA" (Gilbert qtd. in rocketboom.com 2005; art_mobs 2004).

Such anti-elitist rhetoric and action are not new. In 1970 Alanna Heiss spearheaded the Institute of Art and Urban Resources, working with the New York City Housing Authority to locate abandoned or repossessed buildings and saving them from demolition. Such places were revamped into studios and alternative art venues, the most famous of these being P.S.1, a defunct public school in Long Island City co-opted for use as an art institution. The Institute received funding from various sources, including the New York Council on the Arts and the NEA, and cultivated audiences drawn from the general public as well as art world initiates. Heiss de-emphasized art's financial aspects and focused on its potential for social commentary and change (Smagula 1983: 31–2, 34), countering officious, unapproachable images of museums with a friendly welcome in more familiar venues. But ultimately, these endeavors remain the purview of people in the loop about the constant flux of art world happenings. Undoubtedly P.S.1 offers an alternative to staid museums, but over time it has become institutionalized too (it is now an "affiliate" of MoMA), and its primary audience is an art crowd. If venues like P.S.1 cannot shake the art world's social boundaries, are there other places where these borders could be, if not completely overcome, at least more effectively mitigated? I keep thinking of the shopping mall.

Academics have probed the mall for decades; debating its use of social engineering, examining intersections of urban planning and retail consumption, and critiquing the capitalist system. Many believe the mall is an unfortunate "cocoon" proffering instant gratification and protecting us from "assorted discomforts" (Huxtable 1997: 107), while others concede that it might be public but is not "communal" (Lippard 1999: 76). Margaret Crawford describes shopping malls as spectacles of accumulated goods, meant to stimulate the consumptive desires of demographically targeted audiences (1992: 3–17). But visits to malls are not so inherently passive, even when our interrelations are carefully managed. Malls bring together people diverse in age, ethnicity, and socio-economic class. They come to shop, but also to interact in social spaces that – whether scholars like it or not – have come to function as town squares in many communities. There is little concern that malls are for us; after all, without our patronage their businesses would close.

74

While this overtly commercial nature can be crass, it is refreshing too: we know what malls want from us, which might help us better determine what we want from them. People often feel comfortable and confident in their actions at malls, which directly opposes how many characterize their feelings when in museums – overwhelmed, intimidated, or unprepared, without mastery over the situation. Not everyone will be more receptive to art experiences presented in the context of a shopping mall, but it seems reasonable to assume that some viewers will thrive without the pressuring weight of museum authority.

As sites for public art, malls strike a populist note. Their business enterprises keep unrealistic utopian sentiments and esoteric academicism at bay, while rendering other egalitarian aims more attainable; transcending museums' perceived elitism while making art experiences widely available. Anyone whose interest is piqued by the art can engage in aesthetic contemplation; those who are indifferent can continue shopping. Self-described "social architect" Dolores Hayden enumerates the difficulties of creating "an American sense of place," proclaiming that malls are "placeless" representations of "the common language of American speculative real estate development ... the production of space as a commodity" (1992: 263). On two counts she is correct: most malls lack architectural distinction, and their tenants are usually focused on less than noble goals. But their familiar vernacular and unvarnished commercialism forge spaces in which a multitude of American ideals are produced and reflected; as such, malls are places where public art could prosper.

While touting malls' advantages as sites for public art, it becomes necessary to acknowledge a related phenomenon – the prevalence of art galleries in them. Personally, I do not object to this other than most of the art sold in these venues is not very engaging; reproductions of Impressionist landscapes, photographs of local landmarks, and colorful abstractions to match the couch. The success of Thomas Kinkade, whose galleries proliferated at malls, is endemic of the situation. His quaint images of stone cottages, arching footbridges, and promising rainbows are easily dismissed as lightweight fluff. But it is not Kinkade's subject matter that is problematic; it is his disregard for viewers' critical faculties. At his galleries and online,

Kinkade provides specific interpretations for his pieces; he more than guides our encounters with them, he tries to dictate these. Although his mass appeal might suggest Kinkade is a populist, he is anything but; in his work meaning is wrought primarily by the artist. This approach inscribes a limited world view on viewers' experiences, which are not encouraged to expand beyond the confines of Kinkade's own imagination. It also assumes that viewers must rely on Kinkade to interpret and homogenize these experiences for them, thereby neutralizing the potential for alternative or less enthusiastic readings of his art.

There is a lot of art in American malls, and much of it is not very good, challenging, or engaging. It is visual Muzak, filling voids in our view and marking meeting points, but unlikely to stop us in our tracks or invite lengthy consideration. With their diverse audiences and ample physical spaces, malls are missed opportunities for public art. Since a mall is a conglomerate of private business interests, which do not want to dampen patrons' consumerism, it is unlikely that socially conscious art exploring issues like AIDS would proliferate there. But this does not mean that malls are unsuitable for public art, just that they are not hospitable to all of it. Some artists have already explored the mall as a public art venue. In 1985 John Kavalos collaborated with "upper-middle-class" New Jersey teens to paint murals in three suburban malls (Cherry Hill, Echelon, and Woodbridge). The project, a joint effort of the Rouse Corporation's Art-in-the-Marketplace and the New Jersey State Art Council's Artist-in-Residence programs, benefited both the participants who learned by doing, and mall patrons who had firsthand experiences with the artists and artworks. There were many repeat visitors, including one elderly man who watched their progress daily. Kavalos provided art history and painting instruction and when completed, the murals were dismantled with sections given to each of the teen volunteers. By teaming up a professional artist with motivated though inexperienced collaborators (and an often accidental audience), Phyllis Rosser contends the project created a "sense of community" in the malls (1989: 132–3), which are often condemned for their lack of social engagement.

As Lawrence Levine reminds us, museums were sites of entertainment and amusement until they became "sacralized" in the mid nineteenth century (1988: 151). Though Phillippe de Montebello, Director of the Metropolitan Museum of Art, worries that museums are less likely to challenge visitors if they are too concerned with attracting them, he perceives the museum's transition from "repository" to "activity center" (2004: 157–8, 160–1). One way in which museums have made this shift is to become more like malls, a transformation often prompted by financial need. Almost every major institution features an array of restaurants, bookstores, and gift shops (regional ones boast similar but more modest facilities). It is conceivable that visitors might not delve any further into museums beyond these amenities, which is troubling; at their most fundamental level, museums are places for direct encounters with art. Yet Gurian believes museums' abilities to attract diverse audiences, build community, and tackle social issues are enhanced through such mixed-use spaces (2001: 99–100, 107–8, 112–13). These can enrich our "total experience" of museums (Hooper-Greenhill 1994: 88); making us feel welcome, providing a respite so we can return to the galleries with fresh eyes, or hosting a good conversation about the art we have just seen. When the increased social dimensions of museums are fully embraced, and the commercial aspects of their existence openly acknowledged rather than downplayed, audiences will be better prepared to participate in their culture.

In the mid 1990s when Kansas City's percent-for-art program was booming, critic Peter von Ziegesar noted that public art had not only "changed the physical landscape" of the city, but its attendant controversies had transformed "the cultural climate as well." He concluded, "For good or for ill, almost every Kansas Citian now has an opinion about contemporary art and is conversant with at least some of its terms" (1995: 55). I suggest there is very little "ill" to be found in this scenario. Kansas Citians participated in critical discussions about the function of art in their daily lives, and cultural institutions such as the Nelson-Atkins Museum of Art directly impacted those dialogues. Although de Montebello does not wish to "demystify" art, insisting upon the "wonder" of its experience apart from the everyday, he urges museums to put faith in the "public's ability and willingness" to share in their missions. To do such is not a matter of pandering to or patronizing visitors, but respecting their aptitude: "To gain and keep the public's trust we must not sell the public short" (2004: 116, 160, 168). In his impassioned plea for social inclusion, Fleming outlined an optimistic path for the museum's future:

> In creating a museum that inspires and uplifts people, that confronts them with ideas, that helps them understand a little more about themselves and their surroundings, you are doing the best a museum can do ... having this aim ... refutes the accusation that, in order to have widespread mass appeal the museum must 'dumb down.' Not so, not if you want to make a difference to people's lives. (2002: 224)

It is neither obligatory nor feasible for museums to entice every individual to partake in their offerings; potential museum-goers must assume some liability if they reject or ignore museums on reactionary bases. But it is the responsibility of museums to extend sincere invitations to the public, and the public's duty to make informed choices when accepting or declining these. The museum needs to lecture less *at*, and converse more *with* its audiences to build a sense of "shared ownership" (Spicer 1994), striving toward "an open dialogue from the start" that is "potentially ongoing, not prescribed to a simple exchange" (Gamble 1994: 22). Only after art museums better combat their elitist reputations, and their audiences overcome lingering apprehensions and anxieties, shall truly public exchanges take place between them.

Chapter 4   Not Quite "Art," Not Quite "Public": Lessons from the Private Sector

As public art was riding a crest of 1980s optimism, Peter Blake assessed its quality as follows:

> The last time good public art was created, consistently, was when the world was run by princes and popes, who selected the artists to make the spaces. Ever since universal suffrage raised its ugly head, we have had nothing but trouble. The only good art being produced, nowadays, is private art – because nobody (except the buyer) ever votes on it. (1987: 287)

Blake's statement is audacious, a nearly wholesale rejection of publicly conceived and funded art. Yet he also makes several astute points. First, the public realm is significantly enriched by private patronage. Second, holistic approaches in which artists "make the spaces" rather than isolated objects might best serve public art. Third, financial autonomy can heighten creative autonomy. While Blake seemed ready to discount the merit of contemporary public art, we ought not to be equally dismissive of the private sector's potential contributions to such art. As Patricia Phillips contends, public art has an inherently private core: "The public is diverse, variable, volatile, controversial; and it has its origins in the private lives of all citizens. The encounter of public art is ultimately a private experience" (1992: 304).

79

Throughout history, individual patrons have funded artworks in public places, for public purposes, or to express publicly held sentiments. Certainly many of these people had narrow tastes or were self-serving rather than truly philanthropic, yet it would be more than inaccurate to claim that no genuinely beneficent public gestures have come through private interests. In this country, as Stanley Katz observed, "Doing well by doing good is an old American tradition" (1984: 35). John Dewey agreed, noting that many private acts "contribute to the welfare of the community or affect its status and prospects" (1927: 13). By sharing their resources and enthusiasm for the arts, private patrons promote regional venues while widening their horizons, and furnish their towns with high-quality artworks. They can also support local or "undiscovered" artists, and provide opportunities for art encounters the public might not have otherwise. Stanley Marsh 3 (he deems "III" or "The Third" too pretentious), a wealthy and famously eccentric patron, offers a prime example of how provocative public art can be when freed from committee votes and public relations mandates. Though unworried about local consensus – in fact he seems intent on fostering controversy – Marsh is a community activist. Supplying his hometown of Amarillo, Texas, with art that cannot be easily ignored, he coaxes his neighbors to debate the nature and function of art in the public sphere. *Cadillac Ranch* (1974), designed by the artists' collective Ant Farm, is the best known of Marsh's commissions. Visible from a busy stretch of eastbound Interstate-40 are 10 classic Cadillacs embedded – nose down, fins up – into the ground, a jarring counterpoint to the land's unyielding flatness. (In 1997 *Cadillac Ranch* was moved to a cow pasture two miles west of its original site to distance it further from the city limits.) A constant stream of visitors (tourists, art aficionados, and area residents) make pilgrimages to *Cadillac Ranch*, leaving their mark in spray-painted epigrams on the readily accessible cars. On my last visit (fall 2006) there were many fresh graffiti tags from the day before, including that by a family for whom a visit to *Cadillac Ranch* became a "quality time" bonding experience. Exhausted spray cans are on the ground, and heaped in a large bin at the pasture's entrance. But the tagging does not indicate a lack of regard for the artwork, in fact, it is welcomed. The graffiti is proof of *Cadillac Ranch*'s approachability and populist appeal. Instead of symbols of wealth and luxury, the Cadillacs are embraced as historic Americana. By forsaking their preciousness the cars become resolutely public, and the audience takes proprietary ownership of the art made for them, actually inscribing their names upon it. In this act *Cadillac Ranch* is not defaced, it is transformed into a civic mascot and popular shrine.

Marsh identifies himself as an artist, and often works with the Dynamite Museum (a collaborative of young local artists begun in 1992) to develop and fabricate his projects. Among the most visible of these are traffic signs placed throughout Amarillo and neighboring towns (some reports claim there are as many as 5,000 of them), each with a unique message. The Dynamite Museum worked with commercial companies to replicate the look of official street signage; diamond shapes sporting block-letters. But their signs bear entertaining, infuriating, or puzzling images and texts, often poking fun at art history's staid conventions. A "low" mode of communication, the traffic sign, is appropriated to make "high"-minded commentary (Fig. 2). Examples include, "MY YOUTH IS SPENT AND YET I AM NOT OLD," and "HE'S EITHER A MADMAN OR A POET," which both seem to refer to Marsh. The signs are not randomly placed; they are installed on private property per owners' requests, though are clearly visible for all to see (Cowley 2001). Art insiders cruise the streets of Amarillo in a sort of treasure hunt, seeking signs that are often owned by those outside the art world's orbit. Thus the signs invert the socio-economic structures that usually govern art ownership: Marsh's personal funds provide free, original artworks to members of the public, which are placed not in city squares but at individual homes. An owner may take a sign with her if she moves, or have it removed for free if she no longer wants it. The signs appear in all kinds of settings, from Amarillo's wealthier to poorer neighborhoods, from the manicured lawn to a liquor store parking lot. Some are tailored specifically to owners; a sign reading "ART's exalted character clears my brain" appears on the property of an art teacher. Not all requests for a sign were granted; Marsh and his minions decided who was worthy, establishing a new caste system; instead of economic clout or your family tree, one's appreciation for the arts, hipness, or endorsement of Marsh's antics was awarded. (Marsh and the Dynamite Museum

Figure 2 Stanley Marsh 3 and the Dynamite Museum. *Road Sign*. Date Unknown. Amarillo. Photographer: Cher Krause Knight.

stopped making the signs a few years ago, and now refer inquiries to a custom sign company.) Amarillo, a ranching community not known for cutting-edge art, has been enlivened, entertained, irritated, and enriched by the eccentricity of Marsh and his projects. Though Marsh sidesteps many conventional public art processes (community boards, permits, fundraising), his projects are fundamentally egalitarian, widening art's audiences. Freed from the constraints of social status and money, people who might have never lived with art now own it.

In Chapter 2 we examined a more standard form of corporate patronage, in which the Equitable Life Assurance Society established its own art collection, hiring professional consultants and employing traditional collection management techniques. In this chapter we turn to circumstances in which the private sphere takes the creative lead, and consider what public art might learn from these endeavors. The entertainment industry is able to bridge imaginative thinking and built reality to create themed environments or UEDs (urban entertainment destinations, as termed by sociologist John Hannigan). UEDs are often immersive environments: instead of audiences negotiating around independent objects, they traverse through enveloping settings. These spaces can cultivate highly experiential relationships with visitors, predicated on participatory interaction, not passive viewership. This chapter prompts readers to expand their definitions of "public art" by including works and places few might consider "public" or "art" at all, which were conceived in the private sector. This is not a matter of redrafting the entire map of public art's terrain but rather adjusting some of its boundaries, which requires us to frame our larger culture as a network of shared and meaningful experiences, instead of a series of "popular" but passing fads of limited quality and substance. Such an approach dismantles some presiding assumptions about the depth and value of consumer culture, and asks us to put aside preconceived notions about places like casinos and theme parks.

Within the private sector are powerful visions and great ingenuity, as well as troubling shortcomings; each helps chart a more populist path for public art. In assessing the history of the American commons, Phillips asserts that it "existed to support the collage of private interests that constitutes all communities, to articulate and not diminish the dialectic between common purpose and individual free wills." She reminds us that the public and private domains are *interdependent* entities, whose "textures" are defined through their functions as "foil" and "complement" to each other (1988: 94; 1992: 296, 298–9). George Yudice argues that the arts, threatened by drastic funding cuts, have become entrepreneurial. Noting that the "public good" is now negotiated between the government, private sector, and civil society, he remarks; "It makes no sense to speak of public and private, for they have been pried open to each other" (1999: 26, 29).

The Art of Entertainment

In *Fantasy City* Hannigan outlines the rise of a "culture of pastiche" with UEDs (theme parks and restaurants, casinos, interactive rides, megaplex cinemas, and so forth) designed for "entertainment consumption" that often emphasize visitor participation. Their roots are in a "golden age" of popular urban entertainments (amusement parks, cabarets, sports stadiums, and the like) that flourished in this country from the end of the nineteenth century until the onset of the Depression. Hannigan argues that these entertainments' developers promoted a view of a public culture that was "attractive, non-threatening and affordable" to a wide cross-section of society, implying that a "good-natured crowd" of different classes would peacefully coexist within "democracy's theater." While social tensions actually persisted, these early entertainments did energize their cities. Likewise, many of today's UEDs were built as redemptive spectacles to reinvigorate stalled regional economies, especially as the manufacturing base faltered across the United States (Hannigan 1998: 1–2, 15–30). Although critics decry the "release from 'real' identities and responsibilities – from the serious stuff of everyday social life" that occurs at places like casinos and theme parks (Lofland 1998: 94), these sites are resonant components of American culture and potentially exciting, though unlikely, art venues. They are frequently proactive, site-specific environments that can be framed as art experiences, and are more welcoming to the general public than many traditional public artworks. Since we do not commonly think of themed environments as art places, and they employ broadly comprehended references, people generally feel less intimidated by and more willing to avail themselves of the varied experiences they offer. At museums, art "floats in its own bathysphere" or is seen in "a situation of seeming alienation" (Stephens 1986: 123); at themed environments artfulness is integral to the total concept. Museums present art in an intensified context of reverent protection, while art in our city squares and streets may seem like afterthoughts easily ignored. But in a themed place all facets (the space, furnishings, decorations, props, food, and activities) are interrelated to produce unified, coherent experiences rather than fragmented ones. Hilde Hein commented that "experiences grow stale" as "their shelf life is brief and the cost of refreshing them enormous" (2000: 147), yet these places repeatedly provide fulfilling experiences for many patrons. It would be astute for anyone interested in public art to discern this power rather than discount its relevance and import.

All of the "art" produced at these venues is not of the highest aesthetic or intellectual caliber, but as Marcel Duchamp proclaimed, "art may be bad, good or indifferent but, whatever adjective is used, we must call it art, and bad art is still art in the same way that a bad emotion is still an emotion" (1957: 818). Likewise Arthur Danto argues, "It is possible that a work might be good public art though bad or indifferent as art, which would then make esthetic criteria irrelevant to the matter" (1987: 91). Although I do not wish to segregate "public art" from "art," nor do I think aesthetic criteria are "irrelevant," there are times when such criteria ought to play supporting roles. Even when themed environments are smartly conceived and artfully designed, their detractors complain they are lowbrow entertainments sidestepping weighty social issues. But entertaining the public, providing opportunities for enjoyment, amusement, and relaxation, is no meager goal. Nor must art be "enlightening" at every turn; some of the least satisfying art experiences are those with a heavy-handed didactic or moralizing tone, which treat viewers as if they are sorely in need of guidance. Yet for critics like Michael Sorkin, the popularity of themed environments is irritating and even threatening. He fears that time and space become obsolete in such locales, and the "genuine particularity" of place is eradicated along with any of its attendant social relations. Sorkin worries that a new kind of city has emerged, focused on consumerism at the expense of democracy. Such a city sports the appearance of endless choices, yet a relentless sameness persists – "a generic urbanism inflected only by appliqué" (1992: xi–xv).

In the legendary essay, "Travels in Hyperreality," Umberto Eco chronicled his travels throughout the US, dubbing it an "America of furious hyperreality" with a pronounced taste for well-crafted simulations. He suggests that precise re-creations (such as the replicated Oval Office at the Lyndon B. Johnson Library, Austin, Texas) function as "absolute fakes," blurring boundaries between reality and imitation, history and reenactment, original and simulacrum. The replica achieves "immortality" through "duplication" as a "full-scale authentic copy ... not the image of the thing, but its plaster cast." But at the theme park and casino there is no attempt to fool us with simulacra as "a substitute for reality, as something even more real," or quell our desire for the "original." Eco is right that the theatricality of these places is meant to stimulate consumption (1975: 6–8, 19, 41–43), but most visitors can quickly perceive the commercialism and make active choices about their levels of participation. In fact, they revel in their abilities to distinguish references to the "real thing" from the thing itself. Themed places tweak simulations with shifts in scale, media, geography, and context while heightening the kitsch factor, so that no actual confusion between the "original" and their versions can exist. As Hannigan surmised, we "'switch codes': participating in a simulated experience and then stepping back and examining the technologies whereby the illusion is achieved" (1998: 69). Rather than spectacle collapsing with cognition of its apparatuses (Saunders 2005: viii), its pleasure is enhanced by our apprehension of it. UEDs provide alternative environments that are inspired by, though not "plaster casts" of, their source material; they do not kill our taste for "genuine" history as frequently charged. I imagine few visitors to the scaled-down Eiffel Tower at Las Vegas' Paris Hotel and Casino, or those who visit the France sector of Disney's Epcot Center, now feel they can confidently check Paris off of their lists of "Places to See."

As Andrew Ross contends, popular culture holds meaning for its users, helping to create "political and social identities, by rearticulating desires that have a deep resonance in people's daily lives." Instead of viewing members of the public as consumers manipulated by government, the media, and culture industries, Ross posits we conceive them as experts in their own culture, making informed choices (1989: 52, 148, 232). Alan McKee agrees, suggesting academics are suspicious of entertainment because they fear it threatens the public sphere by encouraging "intellectual laziness." Scholars perceive culture that is readily accessible as "worthless, because it doesn't require audiences to make an effort to understand it." To make his point, McKee contrasts modernist and postmodernist approaches to culture. He describes modernists as passing "universal judgments" about quality, believing that debased culture is forced on the working classes. For modernists, the means to cultural equality is through established routes of formalized education. On the other hand, postmodernists practice "cultural relativism," assessing each culture on its own terms, with popular culture being as valid as any other. McKee argues in favor of the postmodernist method, affirming that popular audiences "don't passively accept what they're given" but are intellectually curious and proactive: "They interpret (culture) in their own ways and make unexpected uses of it" (2005: 82–7). I concur with McKee. An instructive lead may be taken from the iconic book, *Learning from Las Vegas* (Venturi, Scott Brown, and Izenour 1972). The book was written after its authors, a trio of architects, took a group of Yale graduate students to Vegas in 1968. They celebrated the city's vernacular, even when it lapsed in "good design," and reconstituted pluralist architecture as inclusive, allusive, witty, and meaningful. As such their book offered a populist antidote to rampant modernist pretension without arguing for a dumbed-down culture (Knight 2002), a sentiment which is as resonant today as it was then both for academics and the public at large. As Lucy Lippard once observed, while art is "not just entertainment ... it doesn't *hurt* to entertain people while you're having your say" (1989: 218).

This is Special, I am Special

People usually encounter public art by accident; one rarely goes to a subway station for an art experience, but rather happens upon it while waiting for the train. The converse is true of places like casinos and theme parks; audiences purposefully travel to specific locations at their own financial expense because they believe the experiences awaiting them will be rewarding and worth the trouble, that the designated place is somehow extraordinary. A city square is resolutely communal; all are invited, and yet we may feel unenthused or ambivalent about it, as if it would persist whether or not we were there. But a private space, which may charge a fee that confers a sense of status, can feel both exceptional and hospitable; outside of our daily lives, but intent on pleasing the visitors it needs to survive. Since many entertainment places do not require visitors to have specialized knowledge or particular backgrounds, audiences can be quickly put at ease, feeling confident and appreciated. Though some patrons still find art museums intimidating (see Chapter 3), this reaction is unlikely at a themed space, which may be awe-inspiring or sublime, but rarely unwelcoming. These places employ visual and conceptual vocabularies derived from mass culture, and provide experiential environments; rather than merely existing within a space, visitors activate it. While many public artworks – especially of the "plop" variety – have difficulty engaging people, a multitude of privately sponsored ventures have built and sustained public support. Two points must be underscored here. First, those desirous of making art for "the people" ought to become better versed in those people's varied interests. Second, it is wholly appropriate to draw upon popular culture in this endeavor. This does not signify that pressing social concerns are automatically dismissed; in fact, audiences might be more receptive to serious messages delivered through familiar means.

Earthworks (see Chapter 2, *Art as Pilgrimage*) provide essential cues for comprehending the intersections of private endeavor and public art. First-generation earth artists worked on vast scales, echoing contemporaneous bureaucratic systems and multinational corporations. They operated much like real estate developers, overseeing construction, negotiating with financiers, obtaining land rights, and managing budgets. But they were also community activists, promoting environmental consciousness while enlisting support from local officials and the wider public (Deitch 1983: 86–7). Although their projects brought attention to the earth, they still imposed spectacular built schemes on the "natural" landscape. By either making interventions into or actually rearranging the land they exercised mastery over it, making it "visually manageable" (Baigell 1989: 3, 5–6, 8). Many of these artists pursued private backing, aware that big ideas cost big money. Yet despite privileging an individual artist's vision, and utilizing private funding sources, earth- and site works often held distinctly public aspirations. They brought awareness to previously under-recognized places, highlighted interplay between the environmental and social realms, and promoted "interfacing the environment" rather than apprehending singular objects (Adcock 1990: 44). These artists also defied the self-mandated system of museums and galleries; like good populists, they sought alternatives when the "accepted way of doing things" no longer served them best. With the constraints of conventional art institutions and practices set aside, they cultivated highly personal reactions to art, underscoring "the coexistence of its space with that of the viewer" (Morris 1992: 253). Earthwork artist Robert Smithson called for more temporal experiences with art, acknowledging the ephemeral nature of existence and thought. He argued for "primary envelopment," prompting artists to break the "focused limits of rational technique," shirk studio life's containment, and become one with materials and spaces. Private entrepreneurs may be able to do so more easily: instead of being discouraged by a priori boundaries, they employ creative technological tactics to accomplish novel feats; the scope of their endeavors frequently requires massive scale; and they produce immersive settings for social engagement and aesthetic contemplation that, perhaps unknowingly, upset "our present art historical limits" (Smithson 1968: 84, 87, 89–91). Of course there are major differences here, most especially earthworks' emphases on meditative solitude compared to the carnivalesque atmosphere permeating most themed environments. But both require complex engineering and construction methods, coordinated labor, and cooperative efforts to render the spectacular (Alloway 1976: 51).

Earthworks transform "unmarked land" into "concretized, identifiable, specific locales" merging artwork and setting (Baker 1976: 74–5). A similar effect occurs at themed environments, though most do not begin life as site-specific entities. Although their physical locations may be chosen for topography or climate, themed places often recalibrate or set their own environmental borders, thus reversing the pre-conditions of site-specificity.

Yet a well-themed space becomes site-specific, conveying a sense that no other place in the world is quite like it. While site-specific works counter notions of art as a bauble to be bought and sold, themed places brashly embrace and even foreground their commodity functions. Intentionally or not, these spaces make visible socio-economic and -cultural conditions when we consider how they are used, and who feels able or chooses to do so. Rosalyn Deutsche called for public art that acknowledges both the aesthetic and social uses of space rather than privileging one over the other (1992: 160–1). Themed spaces make these functions complementary, while underscoring the fiscal realities of their existence.

Private spaces are often well monitored and maintained by their owners. More carefully protected from harm or neglect than artworks in the public realm, their specialness is preserved by clearly inscribed borders. Opened in 1971 on what was formerly swampland, Disney World in Orlando, Florida, became the benchmark of themed entertainment. Its delineated boundaries and physical isolation mark a liminal transition from everyday life into its more rarified and vast terrain (some 28,000 acres), which ensured Walt Disney an unparalleled degree of "quality" control. Not only is Disney World guarded, spotlessly clean, and manned by service-oriented employees ("cast members"), but the scale, scope, and detail of every aspect are choreographed to produce holistic, immersive experiences. Magic Kingdom, the first park built at Disney World and that most directly shaped by Walt's vision, is mapped as a radial form. Its layout promotes ritualized progression and leisurely pace, with serial transitions between each themed sector. As such it is a highly experiential, fully enveloping space, which requires both our physical movement in and sensual engagement with it. For example, Main Street, USA is the only path into and out of the Magic Kingdom. Disney's Main Street is frozen in a non-specific and uncritically patriotic past; its "selective amnesia" purges social disharmony and historical blemishes. The quaint, individual storefronts conceal massive, interconnected retail spaces – shopping is the first and last activity of the day. Main Street is laced with wistful memories, most especially those of Walt's idealized boyhood in small-town America (specifically Marceline, Missouri), the celebratory tone of which is distinctly different from the economic hardships

90

his family actually endured. As Michael Wallace suggests, Disney's "approach to history was not to reproduce it but to *improve* it" through a "retrospective tidying up of the past," which is "freely and disarmingly" admitted (1989: 159, 161–2, 167). Thus Main Street functions as a "marinade of nostalgia and sentiment … meant to ostensibly bespeak a kinder, gentler world" (Fjellman 1992: 394). Walt was jingoistic and unrealistic, but sincere; within his insulated world, he fashioned a view of the US free of cynicism and contradictions (Knight 2000).

James Howard Kunstler dislikes Main Street, USA and its "selective style of nostalgia," complaining its underlying message is "that a big corporation could make a better Main Street than a bunch of rubes in a real small town." And yet he admits that Disney's Main Street is visually interesting and has its own charms: "It is a well-proportioned street full of good relationships between its components, and blessedly free of cars" (1993: 220–1, 225). Blake took a less cynical view of the Magic Kingdom. Though not a "real town" as no one lives there, he argues that its pedestrian-packed, human-scaled streetscape is reminiscent of walking cities like Florence, Italy. For Blake, Disney World is "infinitely more 'real'" than so-called "ideal city" planning and its dehumanizing effects (1974: 89–90, 94). Disney's designers, called Imagineers, did not reproduce Marceline or any other town exactly; they sampled from small-town life. Cultural geographer Richard Francaviglia posits that while academics remain rueful of Disney's neatly edited "reality," Walt's vision has "nearly universal appeal." He concludes: "That Disney was 'one of us' is underscored by the mass appeal of his Main Street. We feel comfortable there as we fill the role of consumers of both products and place" (1996: 157, 162).

Disney's critics worry that theme parks will become "indistinguishable from the real world" (Zukin 1995: 58). While Eco asserts that Disney's "magic enclosure" clearly inscribes its function as fantasy, he laments that in perfecting "the fake" Disney "not only produces illusion, but – in confessing it – stimulates the desire for it." Yet Disney's imitations are not as "perfect" as Eco suggests; they are easily identified as simulacra. To partake in their pleasures does not make "reality" inferior, or relegate us to "total passivity" (1975: 43–4, 46, 48). Though Sorkin may have contextualized it as a "utopia of transience" and an "aura-stripped hypercity" (1992: 206–7, 231–2), Disney World is a very real place, not a mutant city-want-to-be, but a theme park proffering its carefully branded, immersive fantasy to a knowing clientele. Disney's historical and fantastic scenarios may be simulated, but the experiences it provides through these are quite real and for some, perhaps, enlightening. Contrary to George Ritzer's assertion that people are unaware of and unable to rebel against the controls exercised over them at Disney World (1998: 144–5), I argue that an increased level of honesty exists there. Since commercialism and fantasy are so inextricably and clearly linked with no serious attempt to hide either, most visitors can readily discern, and accept or reject, the consumptive overtures and Disney's particular brand of fun. Though Lyn Lofland contends that "counterlocales" such as Disney World foster revulsion for "rough-and-tumble reality" (1998: 216–17, 221), she frets needlessly. Disney's patrons are more than capable of both appreciating and scrutinizing its themed environments. To assume otherwise disrespects Disney's public, and discounts the running critiques to be heard between visitors to the parks on any given day.

Spectacle must be kept in check. As Edward Soja observed, "advanced capitalism" produces and reduces space, "fragmented into parcels, homogenized into discrete commodities" (1989: 92). If the "special" is to remain so, we must fortify some borders. Our society is overrun by the pseudo-spectacular, most visible in the propagation of themed restaurants and shops. Fighting for the attentions of similar demographics, these places distinguish themselves by showcasing their supposedly unique qualities. For example Rain Forest Café, which is found at Disney World and numerous American malls, serves meals in a mock jungle setting as pretend thunderstorms roll in each half hour. The Johnny Rockets franchise, which has also proliferated at US malls, proffers 1950s-styled "diners"; music plays on tabletop jukeboxes while waiters draw ketchup smiley faces to accompany your burger and fries. These themes can be fun but are limited; transparent rather than transformative. Hannigan is correct when he claims we too easily assimilate such experiences into our lives. Any era, style, or culture can be "appropriated, disemboweled and then marketed as a safe, sanitized version of the original," which may benefit investors and corporations more than consumers, and generate an unquenchable thirst for ever-novel spectacle (1998: 69–71, 192, 195–200). What makes a place like Disney World special is that nowhere else is precisely like it. If theming propagates at its current rate, the magic of Disney's kingdom could be lost forever. Writing in 1997 Ada Louise Huxtable retained her "right to remain unenchanted" by Disney's "mediocre, shamelessly consumerized" parks (1997: 49, 116, 253). I suggest that each of us reserve our rights to be enchanted, critical, or both.

Open Pocketbook, Open Agenda?

The relationship between art and money has always been present and frequently uncomfortable, a requisite but somewhat unpleasant reality. Yet economics is one of the meaningful tools through which we can understand art in general, and public art more specifically. If places are free to enter, but their users do not understand, appreciate, or feel welcome in them, are they truly public? Might private ventures, freed from the constraints of an imposed egalitarianism, sometimes be more civic-spirited than their typical public art counterparts? Museums and government agencies striving for neutrality, trying not to offend anyone, can promote bland art in the name of political correctness. No such neutrality exists; there is always someone behind the scenes making choices that usually favor her own tastes. Private sector visionaries can openly indulge highly singular points of view. Since there is no pretense toward consensus and an economics-based hierarchy presides, decisions can be made quickly and unilaterally. While a publicly funded artwork may have literally millions of taxpaying owners who have no direct control over it, privately sponsored ventures have far fewer owners with much greater power. Also, public artists regularly face budgetary and community restrictions, hurdles which might be more easily cleared by affluent, well-connected businesspeople. Private patrons hold the purse strings, select those who will carry out their plans, determine sites and materials, have final say over aesthetic matters, and can prioritize their own preferences over the expectations of others. Some persistent stereotypes must be undermined here: artists, especially public ones, cannot be impervious to financial concerns; and entrepreneurs are not necessarily crass and myopic people who lack creative imagination, caring only for money. Commercialism does not automatically beget mediocrity, and mass appeal does not have to bankrupt spirit or aesthetics (Knight 2002).

When artists get involved in private development endeavors, we may fairly wonder if their integrity and vision are constrained. Corporate branding and the megalomaniacal impulses of ambitious entrepreneurs can threaten the most creative and challenging aspects of public life. Although artists capitulate to grumbling patrons in conventional public art practice, such behavior seems more egregious in business settings. Private clients may have very specific plans in mind with little incentive to alter these; public art scenarios are more likely to spur compromise. But while traditional art venues often resist or cannot financially accommodate change, themed environments embrace flux as a necessary factor in the consumer equation and usually have coffers to draw upon. At its most extreme such fluidity is lamentable; rash transformations occur without pause to preserve or understand the past. But in many respects changeability is laudable; underscoring a willingness to periodically assess projects, listen to the public, and adapt accordingly. The most lucrative of private places, without having to scramble for grants and public funding, can build large-scale dreams delivered to audiences with less bureaucratic mediation. Publicly funded projects are subject to the whims of wider bodies of individuals; artists, community members, arts administrators, politicians. In Chapter 1 we encountered Miami Dade County bureaucrats purposely impeding percent-for-art initiatives. There is something insidious in such activities: we expect entrepreneurs to serve personal interests and are appreciative when they also provide societal benefits. But public officials are supposed to put individual motivations aside for the greater good, adhering to systematic checks and balances.

Furthermore, privately funded projects are usually more resilient to criticism, and even censorship. Public outcry, whether well founded or not, can bring the untimely demise of artworks as happened with John Ahearn's *Bronze Sculpture Park* (1991) in the South Bronx. Ahearn was no stranger to the neighborhood; he had worked out of Fashion Moda, an alternative art space in a South

Bronx storefront, eventually teaming with Rigoberto Torres, an employee at a local religious statuary factory. The two did live castings of area residents in plaster or fiberglass that filtered into the public and private spaces of the neighborhood; on exterior building walls, and inside people's homes (casts were often given to their models). *Bronze Sculpture Park*, a commission from the Percent for Art Program of New York's Department of Cultural Affairs, was a solo project made without Torres. Ahearn sculpted portraits of three neighborhood youths; a teen girl roller-skating, a young man with a basketball and boom box, and another young man with his pit bull. But when these took their places on pedestals outside of the 44th Police Precinct, controversy quickly followed. The artist conceived these as "guardian" figures for a neighborhood – of which he was also a resident – that had more than its share of social problems, drugs, and violence. But some community members claimed Ahearn's work perpetuated negative stereotypes by implying these were "the only available image(s) of themselves." As Jane Kramer described the models, Raymond had been in and out of jail, Corey in and out of jobs, and Daleesha in and out of school. Five days after their installation, worried about a racial scandal (a white artist representing black and Latino community members), Ahearn had the figures removed at his own expense. Insisting that his original intention to "offer complications" was wrong-footed, Ahearn said he should have focused on making people "happy" (Kramer 1994: 37–40, 42–3, 131). Did Ahearn act too quickly, too uncritically? Bend too much to the will of some vocal neighbors? Phillips observes that the professionalization of public art is antithetical to the artistic process; to navigate the choppy waters of bureaucracy, artists might forsake their creative edge, producing conformist, predictable projects. She characterizes such as "minimum-risk" art, expected to "engage everyone but seriously offend or disturb no one" (1988: 93, 95). In contrast, private developers are wise to consider public perception, but do not have to buckle under its weight. They reach expansive audiences and often succeed in enchanting them; with autonomy comes the ability to take chances that may not always dazzle, but rarely bore.

In Las Vegas, Nevada, flights of escapist fantasy take physical form. The city's first public art was its 1950s neon signs; easily seen and apprehended advertisements set against low-key buildings (Knight 2002). Though some critics found Las Vegas impossible to rehabilitate, "a town created by gangsters for gangsters" (Kunstler 1993: 134), by the early 1990s "Sin City" made a bid to become a family-friendly destination. This was spurred by competition from other gambling venues and the city's exponential population growth (from 1990 to 2000 it grew over 85 percent, despite a strained water supply, air pollution, and over-development; Hayden 2006). In 1993 three mega-complexes opened, combining hotel and casino facilities with entertainment extravaganzas, The Luxor, The MGM Grand, and Treasure Island. According to Morris Newman, these marked the rise of "Flaming Volcano" urbanism, a revival of Baroque theatricality conceived primarily for pedestrians as "a presence on the street," in which "the building virtually dematerializes behind the spectacle" (1995: 82, 84). Such sidewalk spectacles are privately funded and intended to incite consumption, but interested viewers can watch them for as long and many times as they want, free of charge. For example at the Treasure Island Hotel and Casino, designed by Jon Jerde Associates, a pirate theme reigns, especially in its 30-million-dollar-plus "seaside" town, initially named Buccaneer Bay (Fig. 3). Supposedly inspired by Robert Louis Stevenson's novel and developer Steve Wynn's visit to the set for Steven Spielberg's *Hook*, the Bay hosted nightly shows with special effects, live actors, and pyrotechnic explosions, which culminated in the sinking of a full-size British frigate several times daily. Wynn even marketed the Dunes Hotel's demolition as a media event in which the historic hotel succumbed to phony canon fire from a Bay ship on Treasure Island's opening day (Knight 2000: 303). As David Johnson quipped, "the pirates always win in Vegas" (1994: 35).

Today Vegas once again embraces its reputation as an adult paradise, attested to by its latest marketing campaign: "What happens in Vegas stays in Vegas." While family-friendly imperatives are downplayed, the upscale facilities and over-the-top theming ushered in with the mega-complexes persist. In 2003 Treasure Island reinvented itself as "TI" and renamed Buccaneer Bay to Sirens' Cove; the pirate theme is less pronounced and more "adult." Now the pirates do battle – four times a night – with singing, dancing sirens in spandex. It seems Vegas has a perpetual case of "revisionist flu."

Figure 3 Jon Jerde Associates. *Buccaneer Bay* (now *Sirens' Cove*). 1993. Treasure Island Hotel and Casino, Las Vegas. View in 1998. Photographer: Brooke A. Knight.

With little sentimentality for the city's past or that of his own projects, Wynn is the guiding force of Vegas development: bigger and newer are always better (Knight 2002). Though ever the consummate businessman, some of Wynn's gestures are under-girded by a populist spirit. His 300-million-dollar art collection, featuring works by Picasso, Cézanne, Gauguin, and Monet, is on public view in the Wynn Hotel, also in Las Vegas. Wynn claims that one never really owns art, but is a custodian responsible for its dissemination: "These things should be shared with everyone" (Wynn qtd. in Eastwood 2006: 63).

Though Huxtable insists that Vegas' public spectacles are relegated to "the relative merits of the imitation" (1997: 75), Newman retorts that "the artificiality exhibited in Las Vegas isn't phony anything; it has its own resounding, relentless identity" (1995: 82). It is easy to dismiss Vegas and its public art as commercial, overwrought, lacking nuance. But Vegas is more than "staged

authenticity" (MacCannell 1973), or a stringing together of mean-
ingless encounters with simulacra. Its simulations offer us alternative
experiences differing from their original models, but nonetheless
quite real (Knight 2002). As Newman concluded, while "the taste
level of these ... extravaganzas is often low," they "manage to ani-
mate public spaces and engage pedestrians more readily than the
lifeless 'public art' that litters many major cities" (1995: 86).

Of course the abuses of private patronage are real and numerous,
especially when private interests are disguised as public gestures.
While working at the Philadelphia Museum of Art (PMA), Danielle
Rice chronicled the curious situation when a statue of Rocky Balboa,
fictitious and well-loved hero of the "Rocky" films, was placed at
the top of the PMA's steps (an iconic scene depicted the boxer
racing up these). The work is an over-life-size bronze of actor
Sylvester Stallone in boxing trunks, gloves raised in the air. It was
sculpted by A. Thomas Schomberg, not as a piece of public art but
as a movie prop for *Rocky III* (1982). Yet Stallone wanted to donate
it to the PMA, lobbying to have it become a permanent fixture
there (and claiming to have done as much for the city as Benjamin
Franklin!). A battle played out in the media, pitting the "everyman," as represented by the wealthy movie star, against an elitist
institution – though the property rights were held by the Fairmount
Park Art Association, not the PMA (Rice 1992: 228–35). Eventually the statue was moved to the entrance of the Spectrum sports
arena, and into storage in 2005 when the Spectrum was demolished. Gearing up for the 2006 release of the next installment in the
"Rocky" saga, Stallone and his minions finally succeeded in having
the statue permanently sited at the foot of Eakins Oval, next to the
PMA's steps. In September 2006, only two days after the Art
Commission's vote of approval, the work was already installed,
being unveiled by Stallone at a dedication ceremony. Writing about
the work's new home, Robert Strauss commented, "It may not be
great art, but the sculpture of Rocky ... is definitely a great draw,"
prompting people who would not normally visit the museum to do
so (2006). On the surface *Rocky* seems a populist monument: culled
directly from mass culture, a symbol of the American Dream, and
an instant tourist attraction. But it was neither conceptualized nor
intended to serve as public art. Only after the fact was that function

suggested by a self-aggrandizing individual, attempting to bypass more democratic procedures by proclaiming to know what the public really wants. It is not that every public artwork must start its life designated as such, that only "bona fide" historical events and figures deserve tribute, or that the temple of culture would be sullied by the visage of a humble boxer who made good. But decidedly private agendas should not masquerade as public ones; Stallone used political clout and star power to get his way. The statue is undoubtedly popular, but the conditions of its placement are anything but populist.

Privatized economic agendas can inspire both contempt and trust. On one hand, we are rightly suspicious of entrepreneurial enterprises that exist, seemingly, only to take our money. But on the other, it is refreshing to apprehend the financial parameters of a relationship, and determine how much or little we *choose* to engage accordingly. Some criticisms of private real estate schemes are well founded; entrepreneurs may be far less socially responsible or community-oriented than interested in fiscal profits via good public relations. In "expertly produced, professionally 'humanized' environments" troubling socio-economic and -political dynamics can be neutralized, smoothed under comforting veneers of efficiency and beauty. At their most basic, such places are aesthetic band-aids providing modest amenities and moralist platitudes; they mask but do little to heal social ills (Deutsche 1992: 158–9, 162–3, 167). We cannot expect private enterprises to glow with utopian idealism, promising to make life better for all. But the resources – not only financial – of savvy and intelligent entrepreneurs can produce places that are more coherently conceived and better built than those by their public counterparts. Rather than wallowing in reactionary anti-capitalism sentiments, pretending that money does and should not matter, it is better to acknowledge the advantages of a secure fiscal base without being wooed by it. For example, Christo and Jeanne-Claude reject outside funding to retain creative control of their projects. They adopt (or parody) "corporate structure" to realize vast, technically complex pieces; making extensive plans, commissioning environmental impact reports, running safety tests, identifying opposition, and encouraging "energetic debate accompanied by its share of democratic madness" (O'Doherty

1981: 337). Their tactics quell potential detractors' complaints about public monies being spent on art; in fact, their artwork often jolts the regional economies of its hosts. And since the artists collect no profits or royalties from the brisk trade in "Christo" souvenirs, all proceeds go to charitable causes (van der Marck 1992: 105). In the case of *The Gates* (see Chapters 2 and 6), Christo and Jeanne-Claude not only footed the 21-million-dollar bill, but employed about 1,000 people through the project, and brought an estimated quarter-billion dollars in tourist revenues to New York City. Millions of dollars from the sales of keepsakes and books went to local nature organizations, especially the Central Park Conservancy (the park is maintained through a public–private partnership between the city and this nonprofit). *The Gates* was not designed by committee, though the project required approval from public officials and engendered community participation through its extensive process. The artists circumvented the traditional pitfalls of public art with, as Jeffrey Kastner describes it, a "roadshow … that literally overwhelms a city's own bureaucracy, effectively turning it into a junior partner that can do little more than express gratitude for the couple's gift." By putting "questions of economic self-sufficiency at the very heart" of their projects, Christo and Jeanne-Claude make a case that in the twenty-first century, "the most popular public art" might "necessarily be the product of private enterprise" (2005).

Christo and Jeanne-Claude's work is well respected in the art world, yet this is not their "primary constituency" (Danto 1987: 92). The artists inspire a cult-like following and media frenzy, which they believe serve a higher purpose – the democratization of art – "fighting the good fight against overwhelming odds in order to bring 'joy and beauty' to the world" (Kastner 2005). I once had a student who characterized them as the "Robin Hood of the Art World." It is an apt comparison; they act as their own art dealers, selling their preparatory works and early pieces from the 1950s and 60s to fund large-scale projects available for free to everyone. Christo and Jeanne-Claude delicately walk the line between public and private, indulging "our poetic imagination" while "exploiting … the capitalist system" (van der Marck 1992: 105). When the role of money is held in balance with art's other components, we can better delineate the purposes art serves, and decode the messages it sends. And as Christo and

Jeanne-Claude prove, artists can even be liberated when they have some power over the fiscal realities with which they must cope.

Embracing Spectacle

Spectacle is enchanting, seductive, engaging, memorable, invigorating, sensual, provocative, and powerful. Even before Edmund Burke sang the praises of the "Sublime" and the "Beautiful" in 1757, there was palpable human desire for transcendental, spectacular experiences. William Saunders identifies two critical camps in regard to spectacle: those who see it as a debasement of genuine artfulness; and those who feel its detractors are too moralistic or naïve to perceive spectacle's import (2005: viii). In the Age of Enlightenment, architects like the Frenchmen Étienne-Louis Boullée and Claude-Nicolas Ledoux designed geometrically austere, romantically surreal, and fantastically grand buildings, many too ambitious to be built. These comprised an *architecture parlante*, "architecture that speaks" its character and function, which became the spiritual precursor of built spectacle two centuries later (*Visionary Architects* 1968). Scott Bukatman traces the origins of contemporary spectacle to eighteenth- and nineteenth-century paintings, which proffered "hyperbole of the visible." Such works emphasized the pleasures of "scopic mastery" and "panoptic power" over simulacra (Bukatman 1995). Simon Schama acknowledges similar tastes for spectacle, citing numerous examples of "designed excitement" in eighteenth-century European gardens. Here affectations of natural growth were achieved through mechanical means to produce *fabriques* (synthetic landscapes), which exuded an "air of unapologetic artificiality" (1995: 540, 559). For Guy Debord, a key member of the Situationist International (see Chapter 5), spectacle's evolution in the twentieth century threatened culture. In his view, lived experience was in danger of being edged out by simulation, with commercialized fantasy usurping intellectual and socio-political engagement (1967). Artist Martha Rosler aptly reminds us to be wary of spectacle's seductive powers, which can divert attention from pressing social matters. But when she delineates the differences between an "audience" that consumes spectacles, and a "public" that engages in a "space of decision-making" (1987: 9–10, 14–15), Rosler neglects to consider that spectacles might have the capacity to cultivate proactive "publics." The spectacle is not a preference for "the simulation to the reality" (Sorkin 1992: 216). It augments rather than replaces daily existence and has value beyond satisfying momentary cravings; meeting longer-term needs for profound experiences, spectacles can take up permanent residence in our memories. When we hastily dismiss the "wonder" of spectacle as short-lived and of limited potential, we miss out on its residual effects, spectacle's "resonance" (Greenblatt 1991: 42). Admittedly, many spectacles are unable to make the transition from inducing awe to sustaining meaning. But those decrying spectacle's "artificiality" need to recognize that throughout history, our environment has been shaped by more than geological forces; human cultivation turns "raw matter" into built landscape (Schama 1995: 7, 9–12). Central Park, designed in 1858 by Frederick Law Olmsted and Calvert Vaux, is a carefully plotted sequence of artful vistas. Significant funding (14 million dollars) and Herculean efforts (moving 10 million horse-cart loads of earth) were required to evoke its "natural" beauty (Smithson 1973: 123; Schwartz 2000: 76).

The "visual enrichment" of our cities and towns remains a consistent concern (Beardsley 1981a: 10), as critics worry that our "built record" is being sacrificed to regentrification (Huxtable 1997: 15, 95–7). In her study of shopping malls, Margaret Crawford maps a "retail drama" in which the theatrical production of space incites consumerism. She claims the "festival marketplaces" of James Rouse (these include Boston's Faneuil Hall, Harborplace in Baltimore, and New York's South Street Seaport) so thoroughly blend "genuinely historic and scenic places" with generic consumptive impulses that "authenticity" and public space are lost (1992). M. Christine Boyer concurs. In her scathing analysis of the Seaport, she describes a manipulative spectacle, descended from nineteenth-century shopping arcades, dioramas, and world's fairs. She frets that despite efforts toward coherency the Seaport's fragmentary, "artfully composed historical ambience" will completely obscure the "real" and gritty past of the site. Boyer's concerns about opportunistic consumption, short-sided development, socio-economic inequities, the privatization of public space, and preservation of social and physical history are well founded. But her argument privileges the Seaport's older identity (working-class fish market) over its perpetually evolving new ones (corporate hub, regentrified neighborhood, tourist attraction). She assumes the recent past, inherently less "authentic," cannot compare to the distant one; implying that visitors "scarcely aware of how relics of the past have been indexed, framed, and scaled" are neither savvy nor bright enough to comprehend the liberties taken with history. Thus, when lamenting the spectacle as "a bracketed moment" (1992: 181–5, 189, 191–2, 204), Boyer forgets that history itself is highly edited, and that she too is one of its editors. Despite her concerns that living history museums and restored historical sites are more likely to produce memory rather than "reclaim" it, Barbara Kirshenblatt-Gimblett underscores their populist underpinnings. Such places allow their publics to "actively engage the site and those in it" while the "virtual world they are exploring pushes back" (1998: 187, 192, 195). In such situations experiences are paramount over objects, and the audience members become "cocreators of social meaning." As Spencer Crew and James Sims claim, "authenticity is located in the event" (1991: 174).

One way hesitant observers might become tolerant of themed places, if not actually fond of them, is through recognition of their capacity to foster critical engagement. Usually such environments are characterized as unchallenging; unwilling to consider difficult issues, or encourage visitors to think for themselves. Many private ventures try to distract us from worrisome or ponderous thoughts that might cause us to close our pocketbooks, yet they still invite analysis from wider populations in a way the art world cannot. Many people quickly and effortlessly launch into impromptu critiques about their experiences at themed places because they feel more welcome and expert to do so. If the art world could put its potential audiences equally at ease, there would be much richer analytical dialogues. Instead critics and art historians address tight circles of insiders, or at the broadest scope, self-identified art enthusiasts. As stated in Chapter 3, the role of specialized knowledge is essential in art, but it becomes limiting when too many people feel discouraged from interacting with the art and institutions supposedly meant for them. Some members of the art community still look at the public at large as a problem to solve, or too simple-minded to really understand art. Conversely entrepreneurs often give audiences more credit, assuming we will perceive this and "get" that. Even those unfriendly to capitalist rhetoric and tight social management admit there is something to learn from well-organized, efficient, visually pleasing, and crowd-controlled places like Disney World. In Wallace's examination of historical re-presentation at the Disney parks, he found an overly optimistic, at times "profoundly distorting" and "commercialized history," but also imaginative techniques with the potential to teach "people more history, in a more memorable way, then they ever learned in school, to say nothing of history museums" (1989: 158–9, 162, 173–4, 178–9). If visitors are provided with critical tools, they can detect historical mutations and challenge hierarchical agendas.

Some critics will surely bristle at the suggestion that themed environments proffer art experiences, complaining about a lack of aesthetic virtue and intellectual rigor. But it is hard to discount these places' ability to create popular, social spaces that have meaning for their users. Many public artists are now conceiving holistic spaces rather than producing discrete objects; providing retreats from the hustle of daily life, lively places to congregate, or alternatives to the ordinariness of one's usual activities. Themed environments are conceptually similar, and often succeed in attracting people and encouraging repeat visits through their efforts at community building and social engineering. It is instructive for public artists to study such private ventures. When assessing what she termed the "new public art," Rosalyn Deutsche was wary of its supposed social responsibility (1992: 1996). But themed spaces avoid a major pitfall of this "new public art"; they do not merely graft art onto a social milieu, but merge these in a fully integrated entity. Every aspect of the entire space is purposefully artful and engaging, prompting frequent social interactions among visitors. While these may be of a limited nature ("Can you take our picture?" or "Do you know a good restaurant around here?"), they are nevertheless sincere. Such exchanges bespeak mutual trust and camaraderie, encouraging individuals to participate in communal networks.

Spectacles are sensory; they require us to enact and experience rather than passively receive. The traditional art world remains primarily a climate of sight, despite many efforts to rebuke that myopic orientation. Themed environments ask us not only to see, but to continually touch, taste, smell, and hear. They are more immersive than most installation art (still bounded by art institutions' physical and conceptual frameworks), and their visitors have fewer compunctions about fully engaging with them. Themed places extend life experiences rather than art-specific ones. As a form of contemporary spectacle, they empower people to feel confident in their perceptive abilities, providing cues that bring our attention to noteworthy elements while discretely gleaning over those deemed less "interesting." While this editorial function is potentially quite controlling or troubling, it also enables designers to coordinate the spirit of a place to the activities undertaken there (Wagenknecht-Harte 1989: 50), helping visitors make dynamic use of the space and discern its tangible connections to their lives outside of it. Privately funded spectacles also dispense with the fiction of universally held beliefs, while at the same time underscoring which values and interests are shared by a particular group or culture. At Disney World, Walt's individual viewpoint became the defining force for its celebration of wider "American" ideals: freedom, creativity, family, nostalgia for the past, appreciation for innovation, love of nature, and respect for history. It would be absurd to claim that such values are uniquely American, but at the same time Disney World's continued popularity indicates that these messages strike a chord with audiences, especially native ones. Dolores Hayden insists that "an American sense of place" and a "common language" are difficult to develop (1992: 261), yet Disney World seems to have forged both. Hayden would surely be unsatisfied with Disney World's commercialized offerings, but it is clear the place has cultivated specific themes that are intelligible and appealing to wide and varied audiences. Cesar Trasobares, former executive director of Miami Dade County's Art-in-Public-Places program, characterized public art as embodying a "shared vision" for a place in the "desire to showcase human aspirations and human expression" (Trasobares qtd. in Joselit 1990: 183). Admittedly, not all of us share in the visions of people like Disney and Wynn, but it cannot be denied that they have created stages upon which cultural aspirations and forms of expression are put on view. Themed environments are rarely discussed with ambivalent indifference; they may be objects of unbridled affection, or endure mockery and degradations of their worth, but both the adoring praise and sharp criticism attest to their power. Spectacles stir emotion and spark debate, as does the best of public art.

Chapter 5   Super Viewer: Increasing Individual Agency on the Public Art Front

One evening in 1987, an attendee at a "Town Hall" meeting hosted by the Dia Art Foundation asked how art might engage wider audiences without becoming "watered down." Artist Barbara Kruger, one of the panelists, responded:

> We should think about this notion of watered-down culture – this idea that as soon as production gets pulled away from the institution, its power and money, it becomes watered-down. It's a literal description: as the opposite of "rich," "watered-down" suggests a loss of wealth, of value. But it's not necessarily the case. (Kruger qtd. in Foster 1987: 51)

This exchange underscores the persistent gaps and power struggles between arts professionals and institutions, and members of the public. Given these underlying tensions, Erika Doss suggests we should not be surprised when people "view public art as both irrelevant and a blatant symbol of their loss of autonomy in the public sphere." Instead of apprehending public art's capacity to foster cultural democracy, we heap our collective frustrations on it as "a solid, knowable target" (1995: 16–17, 21, 23). Steven Dubin agrees, noting that art can become a "convenient scapegoat," which "acts like a magnet, attracting scraps of civic discontent" (1992: 41). Unless the agency of audiences continues to grow, such discontent is likely to fester.

It would be preposterous to proclaim that an artist's intentions do not significantly impact the interpretation and relevance of her artwork. But we ought to be mindful of allowing artists' views to override any others, or assuming artists were unaware "that they were launching an object into a long and complex journey in which it might be changed in both physical appearance and meaning" (C. S. Smith 1989: 20). Knowledge of an artist's wishes can illuminate our understanding and appreciation of art, but as Lawrence Alloway reminds us, the artist "is not necessarily the sole judge of how it is best seen, or even of what it means" (1976: 225). Even if an artist wanted to control viewer experiences, each of us has our own thoughts, and may be unapprised of or knowingly push aside the artist's intent in favor of personal agendas, values, and tastes. Marcel Duchamp noted that the artist's role was ultimately limited; one could make work, but never impose interpretations. As Duchamp saw it, the artist is unable to fully express or realize his purpose; he needs "spectators" to forage potent meanings unintentionally left in the art (1957: 818–19). Artists are not islands unto themselves. Despite any lingering antisocial stereotypes or proclamations of being unaffected by critics and the public, most artists do care what other people think, which is why they show their art in places where there are larger audiences. This is especially true of public artists, who can benefit greatly from speaking directly with and listening to their viewers. Yet they need not disavow their individual modes of self-expression, or avoid the difficulties that come with deciphering multiple aesthetic and cultural dialects in the public sphere. Initially eliciting positive responses may not always be the most desirable outcome; public artworks that first disturb and provoke are likely to start conversations over topics that are too easily ignored. Had John Ahearn's bronzes in the South Bronx (see Chapter 4) been in place longer than a few days, might the community have grown accepting or even fond of them? Or if the figures were removed after a longer period of time, could honest discussions about racial stereotypes, police relations in the neighborhood, and community self-image have ensued first? The now beloved *Washington Monument* was once the object of scorn and contempt, so much so that citizens halted its construction, dumping stone slabs from the site into the Potomac River. For nearly 40 years the monument

108

remained unfinished, until Congress reappropriated funds to complete it, though matching stone was no longer available. (Careful viewers can perceive a tonal change in the stone as "a faint reminder of the confrontation of one artwork with its public"; Allen 1985: 248.) In another example, a disgruntled graffitist inscribed Richard Serra's *Wright's Triangle* (Western Washington University, Bellingham) with a revealing epitaph: "Art is best when it has been defaced – i.e. demystified" (Beardsley 1981b: 45). Rather than falling in step with an "art is good for you" agenda, this critic expressed dissatisfaction with the perceived pretenses of a self-serving art world. As Rosalyn Deutsche asserts, democracy exists not when conflict is settled, but when it is sustained; "far from the ruin of democratic public space," conflict is "the condition of its existence" (1996: xiii, 270).

Miwon Kwon outlined a three-phase evolution for site-specific public art that explicates the incremental trajectory of audience involvement. She identifies the first phase as art in public places, exemplified by 1960s "plop art" (see Chapter 1), when famous artists – usually male Americans or Europeans – made gigantic masterworks as "antidote(s) to ugly urbanism." Thought to be "site-specific" because it was outdoors, such work actually demonstrated an "emphatic indifference to the site." The second phase witnessed the development of art as public spaces that could be entered, addressing the issues of accessibility on a physical level. The functionality of art was emphasized, and in some cases art was so fully integrated into its site that the two became indistinguishable from each other. The third phase, art in the public interest, ushered in a wave of populist-spirited art, sometimes called "new genre public art" or "community art." Politically conscious artists focused on the socio-cultural dynamics of particular, often marginalized, populations, embracing process-oriented and collaborative methods. This phase has a decidedly activist bent, though Kwon notes that despite its "grassroots" origins such art has also become institutionalized (Kwon 2002; Arning, Chin, Jacob, and Kwon 2006). This last phase sets the stage for our subject here; the increased agency and empowerment of the public. Throughout this book I have aligned the forces of populism with artworks that are particularly experiential in nature, providing opportunities for high levels of participation and interaction. This chapter considers situations in which viewers define "art" on personal bases, determining the scope, value, and type of art experiences to be had. Whether participating in organized collaborative efforts, or constructing one's own social narrative through personal experience of public space, individuals adapt art for their own purposes. As artist Maria Gee observed: "Public art in the past has been used to inform and educate the public. Now the public is being asked to inform and educate the public art process" (1995: 65).

To apprehend the function of populism in public art, we have considered placement, funding, and subject matter, and emphasized issues of audience engagement. The last is paramount here. Populist art is genuinely inclusive of a broader range of people, which does not necessarily mean that its edge is softened, its content tamed, or that it pleases huge audiences. Rather, as framed here, populism is a matter of providing people with the means to feel confident in negotiating relationships with art on their own terms. When Patricia Phillips asserts that public art "need not seek some common denominator or express some common good to be public" (1992: 297), she understands that collectivism does not automatically beget populist results. Populism is not always communal, although it calls for deeper awareness of our social relations. It is also not anti-individualist; in fact at its fullest, populism encourages independent exploration, development of personal viewpoints, and critical interrogations of our public and private selves. Ultimately, populism advocates for the free will and informed decision-making of individuals. Phillips conceives public art as dynamic and active, "rather than a stable collection of formal characteristics," a view which increases the agency of viewers, "who shape, modify, perpetuate and complete" art's meaning. Yet she insists "public art does not need to be user-friendly to succeed" (Phillips 1999). I would add that at its most public, art extends opportunities for engagement but cannot demand particular conclusions, or even expect its overtures to be accepted. Public art need not become "user-friendly" in reductive ways, making things intellectually easy and emotionally comfortable, but rather "user-friendly" in a more complicated sense, empowering individuals to make choices without constantly second-guessing their abilities to do so. Once this happens, it does not matter if the viewer is ensconced within a clearly demarcated art space or happened upon an accidental artwork; her more finely tuned instincts shall discern the "art" in her experiences.

Harriet Senie rightly insists the public is not some passive monolithic group, but comprised of individuals who "reframe" art to fit their needs: "Far from being perceived as an imposition of power, public art is adopted or adapted according to audience activities and inclinations." Thus public artworks become photo-ops, seating spots, meeting places, and civic logos, underscoring perceived deficiencies in the built world and social realm. Senie urges that we not underestimate these viewers, who are insightful, opinionated, and curious, often eager to know more about the art. She concludes: "Although this audience may not be the one envisioned by artists and public art administrators, it is a proactive, potentially responsive, but thus largely untapped, audience" (2003: 188–90, 197).

Power to the People

By the 1970s, fully engaged in the climate of civic activism, many American artists cast off modernism's elitist pretensions in favor of a more inclusive approach known as pluralism. At its worst, pluralism seemed to dull art's cutting edge. Since it accepted all forms of artistic inquiry but was unwilling to subject these to quality judgments, pluralism was hampered by its too broadly defined egalitarian sentiments. But at its best, it represented a genuine democratization of the arts, giving viewers more proactive roles. Though pluralism waned in the early 1980s, many artists still rebelled against what they perceived as a self-indulgent art world, and made art that directly addressed current social issues. According to Steven Dubin, this emphasis on socially charged content allowed artists to speak with new audiences instead of continuing to "talk amongst themselves in a secret tongue" (1992: 25). In *Art in the Public Interest*, Arlene Raven builds a case for public art that is "activist" and "communitarian," though she acknowledges the difficulties in assessing such art, especially when collaborations with

111

non-artists produce work outside of established standards. She mused about how one might separate good intentions from the value of the work. Just because artists or programs seek to do "public good" does not necessarily mean their art will capture the imagination of or resonate with its intended publics, or that it is effective on aesthetic or socio-political terms (1989: 1–2, 26).

Joseph Beuys' notion of "social sculpture," that art could be process and social exchanges rather than product, was realized in the "new genre public art" that evolved in the 1960s and 70s, and gained currency in the 80s. New genre public art eschews modernist celebrations of heroic artistic genius and marketability to emphasize more socially-conscious and -responsible approaches, in which "the reception of public art is as important as, and linked to, its production" (Miles 1997: 8, 12, 14). The goals of new genre public art were most famously articulated by Suzanne Lacy, who defined it as "socially engaged, interactive art for diverse audiences," with roots in leftist and identity politics, and social activism. It is distinguished in form and intention from conventional public art (location-dominated, object-centric, and assuming a generalized viewership), through collaborations between artists and "broad, layered, or atypical audiences." Conceiving "art as communication," new genre public art seeks to move beyond metaphorical investigations of social issues with the hopes of empowering often marginalized peoples. Rather than authorities imposing agendas, artists function as agents for social change, seeking democratic models to share power. Artists work with specific communities (who help develop the terms of the projects) for sustained periods of time, addressing issues of interest to those constituencies. While new genre public art may have a pedagogical aspect, it is not "doctrinaire," and its generally optimistic nature is still "tempered with political realism." The strategies and forms it adopts can blur the lines between art and social work, though Lacy insists new genre public art should not forsake aesthetics for politics, but labor to reconcile these. She concludes that even when it succeeds in bringing social change, this art cannot be measured by "concrete results" (1995: 11–47).

Culture in Action: New Public Art in Chicago (summer 1993) provides a compelling case study in the practice of new genre public art. This program (Eleanor Heartney correctly maintains that the term "exhibition" does not quite fit here; 1993: 46) was organized under the auspices of Sculpture Chicago, a private nonprofit known for commissioning more traditional art. According to its curator, Mary Jane Jacob, *Culture in Action* "aimed to bring into being public art that was as much about the public as about art." The intent was for art to permeate our social systems through process-based projects of an "audience-generated and audience-responsive orientation" (Jacob 1995: 58–60). The program's emphasis on collaborative process over finished product marked a transition in the role of the artist from "a producer of aesthetic objects" to "a cultural artistic service provider" (Kwon 2002: 4). Moving outside of conventional art institutions, *Culture in Action* targeted "audiences that do not typically engage in traditional art museum activities" to foster their active participation in communal endeavors that could have ongoing effects (Corrin and Sangster 1994: 31, 34–5). Jacob emphasized giving voice to community members from projects' earliest stages, rather than foisting ideas upon them from proselytizing, if well-meaning, artists. She contended this forged an open dialogue, a "two-way process of familiarizing and educating; for the artists, to listen as well as speak; and for the public, to make itself known and to learn about itself" (Jacob qtd. in Ramljak 1992: 22). The eight *Culture in Action* projects represent what Allison Gamble describes as "a splicing together of ... the site-specific integrationist approach ... and the socially specific interventionist practices of political and oppositional artists" (1994: 18–21). For example, there was Lacy's *Full Circle*, which focused on the social contributions of women and culminated in a dinner party attended by an international group of prominent women to discuss feminist issues (Lacy encouraged other women to host similar meals). *Flood: A Volunteer Network for Active Participation in Healthcare* was organized by the artists' collective Haha. Located in a neighborhood with one of the highest incidents of AIDS at the time, this storefront hydroponic garden became a physical and symbolic metaphor for the care with which AIDS patients need to be treated. This "high maintenance art," as Haha member Wendy Jacob calls it, provided vegetables and medicinal herbs to AIDS hospices and agencies, and hosted weekly discussion groups on issues attendant to HIV and AIDS. *Flood* was even funded by a local bank for an additional year after *Culture in Action* ended (Arning, Chin, Jacob, and Kwon 2006). To help audiences navigate the shifting terrain of such new genre public art, Sculpture Chicago organized an ongoing series of events beginning about five months before and extending about three months after *Culture in Action* respectively opened and closed. It also offered weekly bus tours and self-guided maps for visitors.

Artist Doug Ashford, best known as a member of the now defunct collective Group Material, is encouraged by tactics such as those evidenced in *Culture in Action*. His enthusiasm is not because collaboration is predictable or "easier, but because there are opportunities to learn," and "people discover a creative context in daily life." Yet Ashford reminds us to be wary of the "dark side" of such community-based projects, which can be reorganized "into a kind of measurable service economy that's based in social effect and urban development" (Ashford, Ewald, Felshin, and Phillips 2006: 63, 70, 72). Eleanor Heartney also welcomes democratically minded opportunities to close gaps between art and non-art publics, commending *Culture in Action* as an "experimental lab." Yet she is wise to ask if any contradictions exist between the social purpose of such participatory art and its institutionalization. She worries that in romanticizing notions of "community," artists neglect "the real tensions and conflicts that underlie any group interaction." Heartney fears an extreme dematerialization of art might occur through such practices, eradicating the distinctions between public art and social activism. She queries, "If we reduce public art to the role of promoting community self-esteem, have we come that far from the false consensus implied by the traditional war memorial or the public statue?"(1993: 46, 48–9). Likewise, concerns were raised about whether some of the *Culture in Action* artists had any sustaining "lived knowledge" of the communities with which they worked, and that the longest-lasting effects from the collaborations were felt by the art world, not the participating communities (Hixson 1998: 49). While the eight projects lacked coherent interrelationships, and their efficacy as collaborative endeavors was difficult to assess, *Culture in Action* still provided an important model for community participation in the arts. It underscored the importance of different ethnicities, races, and cultures having a say in their own representations, without pigeonholing them through limited definitions. Artists spent at least a year collaborating with various constituencies to address their social concerns. As Gee suggests; "Getting input from people rather than simply approval or support raises the stakes ... because it raises expectations that input will be considered, but more than that, acted on" (1995: 64). It is not incumbent upon public artists to become politicians, glad-handing and ever-bending to community whims. But those who engage in sincere interactions with their publics are more likely to gain useful information, wider endorsement, and perhaps some dedicated new collaborators. With the loosening of an artist's controlling grip comes viewers' increased agency in determining the quality and substance of their own art experiences.

Claiming Space and Place

With the rise of activist art groups such as the Art Workers Coalition in New York City, and a new-found appreciation for "community art," inclusive, experiential models for artmaking evolved. This climate prompted the public to actually become artists, or at least work with them directly (Raven 1989: 4, 18), blurring the lines between artists and audiences. The efforts of so-called "outsider artists" are instructive here. These artists are self-taught, and, unless co-opted by the museum and gallery system (as has been the case with Howard Finster), function outside of the art world's conventions and constrictions. "Outsiders" make art for highly personal reasons that often have little to do with fame or money; it was only after Henry Darger's death that his work was discovered and became publicly known. Though sometimes their visions might seem out of step with society at large, these "outsiders" can serve as prime examples of individual agency in the arts, translating personal experiences into publicly resonant ones.

Though a professionally trained artist, Charles Simonds' work is indebted to this outsider spirit. His miniature *Dwellings*, hundreds of which sprouted up like clusters of mushrooms in New York during the early 1970s, offered an antidote to "megalomaniac and materialistic civilisation" (Dimitrijevic 1987: 46). Although the first of these were built in his studio, the *Dwellings* quickly migrated outdoors to SoHo's streets. After 1972 Simonds moved the project to the Lower East Side, bringing art to audiences the art world had largely disregarded (Lippard 1977b: 44). Inspired by Pueblo Indian buildings he had seen as a child, the artist would laboriously erect elaborate structures, spending no more than a single day at a particular site. City streets, cracked walls, building ledges, gutters, and vacant lots playing host to his *Dwellings*, which were sometimes left in deliberately unfinished or ruinous states. The *Dwellings* were intended to shelter Simonds' "Little People," an imaginary community about which the artist had written extensively. The Little People became a poignant metaphor for area residents, struggling for survival under perilous circumstances. Simonds encouraged his audiences to have firsthand encounters with the work, welcoming curious passersby to chat about the *Dwellings* or even help build them. The diminutive structures, constructed of tiny unfired clay bricks, were decidedly vulnerable, both to the elements and anyone who wished to destroy them. As such they became symbolic of the urban fabric; its "inconvenient" or "invisible" citizens (the poor or homeless), the fragile ebb and flow of neighborhoods, and the ephemeral nature of life itself. The *Dwellings* also suggested hope; although some were quickly demolished, new ones would pop up, while still others persisted under the protective gaze of a community. Since the *Dwellings* could not be moved without being destroyed, they reclaimed social space without being co-opted for personal ownership. Thus they became communal property, entry points for discussion about larger social issues, and sometimes sources of pride (one work even lasted for a period of five years; Smagula 1983: 294–9, 304). Bringing the *Dwellings* indoors, as happened at the Whitney Museum of American Art, alters their allegorical and physical context significantly. Here *Dwelling (Part III)* was tucked into a covered niche in the stairwell, no longer exposed to the ravages of weather or available for participatory exchanges with viewers as were its companion pieces across the street. While the indoor work may be preserved, our agency has been constrained to more passive looking. On the street, one could ignore, damage, admire, or safeguard the *Dwellings*; they may have been less precious there, but they were certainly more potent.

By the early 1970s the United States witnessed the rise of two related though distinct movements: muralism, as officially endorsed by local communities, governmental agencies or private patrons; and graffiti. Murals (large-scale paintings, most frequently found on walls) that recorded local events and people, and reflected cultural tastes and collective values, became commonplace in public art at that time. Drawing from the protest narratives of earlier Mexican muralism, the history of Depression-era work relief programs, and 1960s activism, these murals were decidedly anti-elitist. As such they were often overlooked or dismissed by critics, with their inconsistent styles and blatant socio-political agendas constituting "a challenge to establishment ideas on what is admissible as art" (Miles 1989: 31). Painted collaboratively by community members, or by individuals functioning as neighborhood representatives, murals could counter the dispiriting effects of downtrodden areas. Many of the muralists had no formal training, and those who did eschewed solitary studio life to enact social change "in the only forum that then seemed viable: the streets" (Cockcroft, Weber and Cockcroft 1977: xix–xx). Although muralism was not confined to the west coast it did flourish there, especially among racial and ethnic communities that had been largely excluded from the art world. *The Great Wall of Los Angeles* (1976–84), for example, was painted under the auspices of the Social and Public Art Resource Center (SPARC). The scope of the project was admirably ambitious: artist Judith Baca directed the efforts of 30 professional artists, and as many as 450 teen workers (some recruited through the juvenile justice system). Together they produced a 13-foot-high, 2,435-foot-long mural spanning the Tujunga Wash flood control channel in the San Fernando Valley. The work depicts the history of California, from dinosaurs to the 1984 Olympics, "from the viewpoint of those usually written out of the histories." The project was distinctly populist. To learn more about California's multicultural character, Baca brought in ethnic historians to address misconceptions as the mural was still being painted. *The Great Wall* was intended to foster individual and collective identity, and integrate art "into the social as well as the physical space of a community" (Lippard 1990: 170–1). The teen workers had input regarding the mural's narrative structure and design, and were paid for their work as a demonstration of their worth to the community. Baca even organized public forums, arranged for job and drug counseling for her workers, and invited guest lecturers to teach weekly classes on subjects such as social history and economics (Doss 1992: 69, 71–4).

Like muralism, the graffiti movement explored the "communal ownership" of public spaces that had been increasingly privatized (Gude 1989: 321–2). Also like the muralists, most graffiti writers (as they called themselves) lacked any formal art training. But writers' work was differentiated from that of the muralists by its often illicit nature. Many graffiti artists painted illegally upon subway cars and stations, or the walls of privately owned places. Though many observers regarded graffiti as intrusive defacement, others saw it as an energizing enhancement of the urban milieu. Furthermore, while the muralists sought broader, more diversified audiences, first-generation writers were an insiders' group; their work may have been seen by a larger public, but its comprehension was reserved for fellow members of the graffiti community. The genesis of New York's graffiti movement can be traced to a specific person and year: Taki 183 (a moniker combining his nickname and address on 183rd Street), a teen who began tagging in 1970. Early on graffiti developed a hierarchy of style and content. Hastily drawn "throw-ups" were placed anywhere, focusing on quantity and visibility. Other "taggers" took pride in more skillful, stylized paintings of their nicknames. Taggers sought to become "kings," expanding their territory by "getting up" throughout the city, and "bombing" subway trains that would travel to other boroughs with their paintings. "Piecers" (from "masterpiece") emphasized quality and distinctive style through carefully painted, usually large-scale images. Both taggers and piecers employed dynamic graphics, clean lines, layering, "and a feeling of spontaneity" (Geer and Rowe 1995). Though writers often worked in crews (groups), there was a perceptible competitive spirit. Graffitists developed their own system of apprenticeship, in which younger, aspiring writers were mentored under their slightly older counterparts. Despite charges that graffiti was an unorganized movement, writers adopted critical practices and peer review that suggest otherwise: they met at "writers' corners" to discuss issues pertinent to their art, and acted as their own curators, photographing and cataloguing their work, while studying art by other writers (Powers 1996).

According to Suvan Geer, graffiti is both a socio-political dialogue and confrontational gesture that "exemplifies and illustrates who's in charge." Rebelling against the capitalist system by adopting its codes, writers took possession of space by marking it (Geer and Rowe 1995). As Hal Foster queried, "In the midst of a city of signs that exclude you, what to do but inscribe signs of your own?" (1985: 48–9). Yet the public at large had difficulty seeing graffiti artists as anything more than criminals. And critics could not translate their art historical language to accommodate graffiti, even when an eager art market enticed the writers to show in its galleries and museums. Bigotry, too, played a role in the critical neglect of graffiti; the majority of first-generation writers were teens from minority ethnic groups and poor neighborhoods. Today writers often collaborate to protect and preserve their culture. God Bless Graffiti Coalition, Inc., a Chicago-based collective, was founded in 2000 to counter "anti-graffiti trends." The group insists that graffiti is like advertising; a means of delivering messages in public space, though the purpose is personal expression rather than consumption (Thompson and Sholette 2004: 71–2).

In the 1960s and 70s the Situationist International, a politically spirited artists' group, posited themselves as cultural rebels challenging the assumptions of everyday life and its institutions. According to Heartney, they "preached the transformation of the city through a revolutionary merger of art practice and social behavior" (1993: 48). Instead of conceiving art as a "specialized procedure," the Situationists called upon members of the public to evaluate mass culture (Wodiczko 1987: 44; Thompson and Sholette 2004: 16). The loudest voice among them was that of Guy Debord, whose Marxist leanings produced an "unsparing critique" of late capitalism and what he viewed as its dehumanizing technology and placating, consumerist spectacles. Debord believed the public was being purposefully distracted from "real" political situations by passive sensory pleasures that discouraged intellectualism and activism (Ross 1989: 111, 209; McKee 2005: 107–8). The Situationists employed two interventionist techniques to remedy this situation: *detourné*, the rearrangement of popular culture's signs to create new meanings; and *dérive*, short meandering walks to reveal the "psycho-geography" of a city while resisting the controls of its planning (Thompson and Sholette 2004: 16). In a similar vein, a number of subsequent artists' collectives conceive art as cultural critique. By the mid 1980s the Guerrilla Girls were directly confronting women's "systematic exclusion … from the hallowed halls of the institutionalized art world" (Dubin 1992: 63). In 1985 the Guerrilla Girls began their assault, launching a poster campaign of "public service messages" that exposed latent sexism and power structures in the art world. Taking to the streets of New York's then-trendy art districts at night, the Guerrilla Girls used subversive tactics to disclose the inequities of life for female artists that existed under a veneer of patronizing niceties. One of the most famous posters, *THE ADVANTAGES OF BEING A WOMAN ARTIST*, enumerates benefits such as "Not being stuck in a tenured teaching position," and "Being included in revised versions of art history." By providing carefully researched data delivered with tongue-in-cheek humor, and naming specific culprits, the Guerrilla Girls sought to shame fellow artists, gallery dealers, and art institutions into better behavior.

As the self-proclaimed "conscience of the art world," the Guerrilla Girls increased their scope to confront racism in the art world, and then other socio-cultural issues in the larger world such as homelessness, AIDS, and rape. The members of the group remain anonymous, adopting pseudonyms (names of female artists such as Frida Kahlo and Georgia O'Keeffe) and appearing in public wearing gorilla masks. Whitney Chadwick suggests this anonymity and the group's collective identity counter the "art world's obsession with individual personalities," while also protecting the Girls' careers from vengeful curators and dealers. The Guerrilla Girls handily overturn "the art world's cool insistence that great art, like cream, inevitably rises to the top" (1995: 8–9, 11). By naming names and citing statistics, the Girls seek not only to reveal inequities, but to correct them. Their tactics "disrupt the surface calm with which the art world generally operates," exposing its "pressure points" and forcing its insiders to "scrutinize themselves for evidence and complicity in perpetuating social ills" (Dubin 1992: 136–7). In many ways, the Guerrilla Girls are the consummate public artists: they work in the public realm; adopt media from the common culture such as posters and stickers; address issues of wider social relevance; demand fairness from institutions disseminating public culture; and invite viewers to be co-conspirators, for example, by signing their names as Guerilla Girls in gallery guest books, so the watch over the art world becomes a collaborative endeavor.

The Boston-area-based Institute for Infinitely Small Things (IFIST) is an offshoot of iKatun, a nonprofit organization whose mission is to "present and support contemporary art that fosters public engagement in the politics of everyday information" (IFIST 2006). The Institute is a purposefully democratic artists' collective; any interested person can join, and a grassroots sensibility reigns. Comprised of a fluctuating, diversified membership (artists, activists, curators, historians, filmmakers, anthropologists, accountants, and computer programmers have been among its ranks), IFIST seeks to make small "disturbances that have a ripple effect." Drawing inspiration from art movements that have coalesced performance and politics including the Situationist International, IFIST posits itself as a "performance research organization"; donning lab coats (symbols of the "absurdity of their authority"), conducting experiments, and documenting the results. The Institute does not presume to activate public space, which is already always activated, but provides heightened awareness of it through their activities. One of its earliest (and ongoing) projects, *Corporate Commands*, initially began as a database to collect corporate advertising slogans stated "in the imperative." This evolved into a series of performances, influenced by instruction-based Fluxus art. Instead of IFIST scripting the directives, these are taken readymade from the corporate world. The commands, which sell lifestyles rather than particular products, are executed as literally as possible, and performed in close proximity to the signs on which they appear. Since these advertising messages are ultimately oblique, however, there can be no single "correct" interpretation. For example, the group performed "Enjoy Life" (Sovereign Bank's slogan) at Boston's busy Copley Place Mall, picnicking, dancing, and frolicking. By doing so they tested the boundaries of privately owned public space; although there was nothing inherently threatening in IFIST's gestures, mall security removed them so that other patrons would not be disturbed. Thus corporate marketing is interrogated and reconstituted as art practice. By taking the commands to the street, the public is

121

directly (and sometimes unwelcomingly) confronted, though the group does not badger those clearly not wishing to engage. IFIST maintains that it does not make the "black-and-white" judgments of traditional activism, but offers "playful" interventions to scrutinize socio-political constructs (IFIST 2006; Sabal 2006).

In its mapping project, *The City Formerly Known as Cambridge* (begun 2006; originally titled *The Initiative for the Renaming of Names in Cambridge*), the Institute provides a framework allowing audiences to determine their own levels of participation. After being asked by the Cambridge Arts Council to create a work in conjunction with the town's River Festival, the group decided to probe the philosophical, psychological, and physical dimensions of place. Members of the public were invited to rename the streets and neighborhoods of Cambridge, Massachusetts (a self-consciously academic town), or leave things as they are. The project acknowledges the financial infrastructures of art and society; although the first renaming of a place is free – a conquest of territory if you will – subsequent renamings require payment (which usually starts at 25 cents and must increase by at least a penny each time). The most frequently renamed locales reveal what seem to be the most prized and contested places within Cambridge, and underscore the consequences of naming that might normally escape attention. IFIST's renaming opportunities are hosted at community events such as a neighborhood block party or farmer's market, where the group sets up its "portable naming studio." To avoid being coercive the Institute does not solicit public involvement, but shares information on the project with interested parties who can self-select to participate. Dolores Hayden's reflections on her experiences with The Power of Place, a nonprofit she had founded in Los Angeles, are applicable here: "Through mapping … it is possible to find out what residents of a city think about the meaning of urban history in their lives and in the places they go. People in a neighborhood have unique understandings of its landmarks … and social organization" (1995: 229). *The City Formerly Known as Cambridge* is an invitation, not a mandate. It does not demand that people do anything, but presents them with opportunities to make changes as and if they see fit. There is an implicit trust in the public's abilities to engage, judge, and inform. Local citizens furnish illuminating details on Cambridge's evolution that would otherwise likely be forgotten. In fact, the conventional paradigm of art expertise is turned inside out: it is the audience members here who are the authorities, the Institute is just a mediator; only with the public's valuable, insider knowledge can the project be completed. All of the renamings are compiled on the Institute's website, which catalogues when they occurred, and provides quotations from those who initiated the renamings to explain why they have done so. These range from declarative statements that snatch space ("My nickname and I am awesome!"), to socio-political agendas laying claim to unknown histories (Harvard Street was renamed for Ann Radcliffe to recognize her support of Harvard University, which exceeded that of John Harvard himself). Once the project is finished, the Institute will publish a revised map of Cambridge (IFIST 2006; Sabal 2006). Of course, names in the town are not going to actually change as a result of this work, though that is not the point. The Institute prompts criticality of familiar spaces to reveal their history's dynamic fluidity, thereby empowering people to make symbolic reclamations of place on highly personal terms.

Dig In

Over the flux of time, our cities morph, sometimes almost imperceptibly and at others quite drastically; no place is timeless. Cities are always changing as structures are razed or built, people migrate between communities, and personal biographies disintegrate and accumulate. As Nick Kaye contends, the assumed stability of site is a falsely constructed notion; sites are ambiguous, unpredictable, transitory, and conflicting spaces, which would remain inert without their users who continually perform in and thus activate them (2000: 3, 5–6). Both Henri Lefebvre and Lewis Mumford emphasized the social dimensions of the city. For Lefebvre the city was perpetually "ephemeral," and the experience of time and space there determined by "the rhythms of the people" who occupy it. He concluded that "the art of living in the city" was, itself, a work of art (1996: 173, 237). Likewise, Mumford touted the "active drama" of life in a city over its "stage-set" elements, insisting that its social functions were even more important than its physical or economic ones. As a "self-renewing organism" of temporal and spatial shifts, Mumford's city transcended the "tyranny of a single present" to take on "the character of a symphony." He proclaimed, "The city fosters art and *is* art; the city creates the theater and *is* the theater" (1938: 3–4, 439–40, 480, 484).

The users of a space are also its producers (Deutsche 1992: 161); without their agency a place lies dormant, awaiting human interactions and interventions to shape it. Urban spaces change not only through the turbulence of collective social forces, but in the accretion of personal experiences over time. Thus these spaces remain impervious to definitive conceptual readings, even when their physical forms seem rigidly fixed. Since its meanings are "produced not given or universal" (Miles 2004: 151), a city can transform what might commonly be perceived as other-than-art encounters into richly artistic experiences for an individual. Large cities in particular provide numerous opportunities for unexpected aesthetic experiences, especially in their "jumbling" of architectural layers that set the past "cheek-by-jowl" with the present (Lofland 1998: 9, 81, 84–5, 183). A person wandering around a city makes countless decisions every day, often spontaneously, about which activities are worthy of his time and engagement. Jessica Morgan argues that our agency need not always be purposeful; some of the most meaningful art encounters are those that are stumbled upon, upsetting our "comfortable assumptions" while proffering only "half understandings." She writes:

> Rather than taking away from the intended meaning, these ... begin to fulfill the communal ownership and collective interpretation that such public works seek to achieve. The mistake of the traditional monument, it seems, is always to assume a permanence and singularity of significance when the real potential of the public site is its changeability and flux. (Morgan 2004: 7)

Many people are likely to balk at the suggestion that a construction site could function as art, yet I would argue such a place has the capacity to foster art experiences for some viewers. The Big Dig in Boston, a notorious public works project, long over-budget and overdue, is an example of an unintended but potentially quite satisfying public artwork (Fig. 4). In this respect the Dig is notable not for its construction feats but rather its state of flux, a prevalent quality of performance art. The Dig's monumental scale, site-specificity, spectacular effects, and emphasis on the temporal and experiential also recall earthworks. Yet as a government-sponsored project it is operated through highway agencies, not art programs, and haggled over by engineers and contractors, rather than artists and arts administrators.

The Central Artery/Tunnel Project (a.k.a. the Big Dig) is a comprehensive scheme of highways, bridges, tunnels, and public spaces, meant to alleviate vehicular congestion and urban fragmentation. Although accounts vary, most trace the Dig's conception back to the 1970s and its planning to the 80s. Construction commenced in late 1991, under the Massachusetts Turnpike Authority. Still incomplete at this writing, the Dig is the most expensive, technologically

Figure 4 Massachusetts Turnpike Authority. *The Big Dig.* 1991–present. Boston. View in 2004. Photographer: Cher Krause Knight.

advanced, and vast public works project in American history. Boston's 1950s Central Artery, built as part of Eisenhower's US Interstate Highway system, quickly proved to be unsafe and inefficient. It also cut a foreboding swath through the city, destroying neighborhoods and disconnecting downtown from the historic harbor; the Dig partially replaces the Artery with an underground highway and green space. Almost every Big Dig statistic is staggering. During peak construction, 5,000 hard hats labored around the clock and 3 million dollars were spent daily, all while the city continued to operate business as close to usual as possible. According to Peter Zuk, former Dig director, "Building this project ... is like performing bypass surgery on a patient while he continues to go to work and play tennis" (Zuk qtd. in McNichol 2002b: 5–6). In addition to persistent construction woes there is the escalating price tag. The total cost was originally budgeted at 2.6 billion dollars in 1983; the Dig is now estimated to cost between 14.6 to 16.2 billion dollars when completed, prompting Representative Barney Frank to quip that it would have been cheaper to raise the city than lower the Artery (Holmstrom 1996). Thus the Big Dig has been cast as a scapegoat; visible proof of wasteful government spending, a project so complex its completion is daunting. Radio deejays lampoon it, newspaper editorials lament it, and politicians attack it. Its alternative nicknames include: the "Big Park" for the traffic jams it creates; the "Big Pig" and "Dig Deeper" for its skyrocketing costs; and the "Big Lie," implying corruption and scandal. But the Dig has its supporters too, especially local businesses anticipating economic revival, and union members earning their livelihoods. Technically it presents a major challenge as workers navigate under, over, and around building foundations, buried wharves, subways, and live utility lines. Former Dig staffer Dan McNichol offers, "Imagine the Panama Canal being built through New York City and you have a pretty fair picture of the project" (2002a: 17, 105). William Fowler, then director of the Massachusetts Historical Society, insisted, "Thirty years from now, no one will remember (the cost), but they will remember the result" (Fowler qtd. in Schneider 2000).

But a meaningful transformation has taken place; the Big Dig has metamorphosed from elaborate eyesore to an object of aesthetic and public appreciation. Bostonians have lived with the Dig for so many years it seems to have grown on at least some of them. Once abject and scorned, the Dig is now a civic mascot of sorts; in fact tours of the Dig became popular with both tourists and curious Bostonians. Not surprisingly, discussions of the Dig remain focused on its life as a construction project, celebrating its triumphant engineering feats and urban planning, or conversely, exposing its political skirmishes and exorbitant budget. If art comes up, the Dig is conceived as a source of inspiration, not as art itself. The official Big Dig website includes an artists' gallery featuring paintings and photographs of it, but other artists were stimulated by the Dig's potential to act as a host for art, such as Ean White, whose *Interstices* sought to blur "the line between public art and public works." White replaced sections of barrier fence with rear-projection screens and speakers, playing video and audio collected from Dig sites. He observes, "the one thing going on that is truly *gesamt* and practically ubiquitous, urban renewal itself, seems unrecognized for what it is – very important art" (White 2005). I agree, but rather than consider works that comment upon the Dig, I suggest we consider that the Dig, on its own, might function as public art.

Most people concur that Boston will be prettier and more livable when the Big Dig is finished. Conceived with an eye toward ecology and historical preservation, its master plan accentuates parks, improved traffic patterns, and air quality. Yet the Dig was most visually arresting in its highest states of flux; juxtaposing new and old elements of the city that jockeyed about conventional notions of "beauty" and "ugliness." While the hulking highway dinosaurs, rusted and lovely, simply cease to exist, new forms were simultaneously stitched into the urban fabric. There is something profoundly beautiful in the deconstruction of an old infrastructure and the construction of a new one, hanging in the balance between extinction and rebirth. And it is not just the physical transformation of the city, but the conceptual one – the awareness that all things in life change, always – that impresses itself upon you. Most Bostonians must interact, avoid, or deal with the Dig in some way, every day. Its function as both a process-oriented earthwork (it was conceived around the time Robert Smithson and Michael Heizer were busy moving dirt and rocks about) and as a performance piece underscores its artistic potential. Images of the corroded "Green Monster" alongside gleaming expanses of fresh cement have an appeal in their own right, but their beauty is enhanced knowing that they are shifting views of short-lived experiences. Maybe the Dig is art by default, or more accurately, art not by design but by circumstance. Its construction has taken so long, its completion so overdue, that people have renegotiated their relationships with it. Instead of passive citizens navigating obstacles, we are performers activating space. This surely happens for the construction workers, whose synchronized movements display the skill, grace, and intensity of really good choreography employed in very dangerous surroundings. But it also occurs for other citizens as Boston literally changes right before their eyes: a shortcut you faithfully traveled home each day is rerouted the next. For all of their careful scheduling, even Dig officials do not know exactly what to expect. Living with the Big Dig is much like taking part in a Happening; a scripted framework of urban planning and social behavior is in place, but how the free radicals will mix and collide in their environment cannot be predetermined.

It is instructive to make a few comparisons between Boston's well-loved Freedom Trail and the Dig here, as both emphasize the agency of the viewer, encouraging her direct exploration of the physical, historical, and social parameters of the city. Walked by millions each year, the Trail is a literally linear tour of 16 historical sites that bring the Revolutionary War "to life." Visitors track a line of red-painted bricks or concrete marking an itinerary that snakes three miles throughout the city. The Trail features sites firmly fixed in the American historical consciousness, like the Old North Church and Paul Revere House, prompting Dolores Hayden to describe it as a "pilgrimage route" (1992: 266). Walkers have some latitude in following the Freedom Trail, choosing to visit all or some of the "official" sites and making additional stops. For example, although not one of the original sites, Stanley Saitowitz's elegant and haunting *New England Holocaust Memorial* (dedicated 1995) was placed adjacent to the Trail as a powerful plea to safeguard freedom for all, and a heartbreaking reminder of the consequences when it is not. (Its location on a busy traffic island immerses viewers in the bustle of life as they simultaneously meditate on the finality of these cruel deaths.) Most Trail visitors seem to seek a sense of accomplishment that comes with "finishing" its predetermined route. This is vastly different from the Big Dig, which chooses us as much as we choose it, and makes no promises for an orderly journey or a tidy conclusion, unsettling the streets and sidewalks Jane Jacobs identified as a city's "most vital organs" (1961: 29). Thus the Dig's beholder is not unlike Charles Baudelaire's prototype of the nineteenth-century *flâneur*, strolling about the city absorbing its spectacles of accumulation and transformation, anonymous among the city's throngs, though perhaps moving at a more intense pace than Baudelaire proscribed. The Situationists' conception of *dérive* described earlier is essential here. While their recommendation to meander through the city "may seem fairly leisurely and not the least bit political, they propose the radical ideal that ways of being in physical space (particularly in the cities) are political acts" (Thompson and Sholette 2004: 16). Like it or not, the citizens of Boston have the Dig literally at their doorstep; not only is it readily accessible, but it is quite hard to avoid, even despite one's best efforts. The Dig may be maddening, but it is hardly elitist, and the public gets to decide how to respond to it.

Deutsche underscores the tensions between envisioning a city as a "transhistorical form, an inevitable product of technological evolution, or arena for the unfolding of exacerbated individualism" with that of an urban space to be understood "just as art and art institutions had been, as socially constructed spaces." In reality both characterizations can coexist, for together they acknowledge the duality of a city as a collective organism, and the ability of individual agency to rupture or take leave of the communal network, if only temporarily. Deutsche insists we must "dislodge public art from its ghettoization within the parameters of aesthetic discourse ... and resituate it, at least partially, within critical urban discourse" to disclose "the existence of crucial interfaces between art and urbanism in the subject of public art" (1992: 159–61). Artist Robert Morris extolled the virtues of the urban site, claiming that its art "presents a sharper critical edge than that which is more pastoral and remote. It is also more public in the literal, aesthetic, and social senses" (1992: 256). The Big Dig is not a respite for meditative transcendentalism, but its vastness does inspire gape-mouthed awe, not at the wonders of Mother Nature, but at the ability of humans to disassemble and then reshape her on a grand scale. As such, the Dig has its historical precedent in eighteenth-century conceptions of the romantic sublime. Robert Smithson observed that the earth is shaped by continual processes of "disruption," and marveled at the "unitary chaos" of industrial-scale construction. He praised such construction's ability to produce accidentally picturesque "ruins in reverse," which unlike the "romantic ruin" do not fall after they are erected, but "rise into ruin before they are built" (1967: 53–4; 1973: 118). For Smithson the "organized wreckage" of "heavy construction" yielded a "devastating kind of primordial grandeur," of which the process is often more compelling than the finished project (1968: 83, 87). I agree. Once the Dig is completed, and its invigorating plasticity settles into the hardened arteries required of a serviceable infrastructure, it will stop being public art. The Big Dig did not start its life as "art," but one might suspect that many of the best works – the most provocative, transgressive, unsettling ones – could have began as unwitting artistic gestures as well. Originally scheduled for completion in 1998, project officials now hope to conclude the Dig in 2007. As a commuter I am ready for the Dig to end, but as a *flâneur* about the city, I will be sad to see it go. No city is ever really "finished," which is hopefully true of any artwork that lives in the public sphere.

Chapter 6 Conclusion: Art for All?

Reflecting on his shift from private studio life to working in the public realm, sculptor George Segal noted:

> Now I have to take people's feelings into account ... I don't have to apologize for having my own opinions, but I do have to start thinking on levels other than my own ... The question is whether you can maintain the density of your subject matter, a decently high level of thinking, and still be accessible to a lot of people. (Segal qtd. in Beardsley 1981b: 44)

These observations are more than revealing about the personal and collective, elite and popular tensions inherent in "public art." By no means has this book attempted an encyclopedic treatment of public art. Neither is it a guide for professionals (Barbara Goldstein's *Public Art by the Book*, 2005, is an excellent example of such), nor a treatise lamenting mass culture. Rather it offers a populist lens through which to consider public art, based on an understanding of populism as increasing viewers' agency through proactive choices. Instead of building a new hierarchy, an extension of public art's current dimensions is proffered, in which the frictions between public and private, and high and low, remain happily unresolved. Rather than measuring "successes" and "failures" in public art, the book has foregrounded issues of audience response, engagement, and interaction, and called for a wider constitution of "accessibility."

Admittedly, these premises require some readjustments of the definition of "public art," particularly in terms of roles to be played by the private sector. But such privatization can threaten the well-being of public culture, as seen in the contradictory promises of "redevelopment" examined in this chapter. To counter this concern, we will next turn to nonprofit organizations, examining their ability to foster healthy public–private partnerships. The discussion of nonprofits also considers the benefits of temporary public artworks, which are commonly commissioned by such organizations. The chapter then takes up two important models for populist public art: the University of California at San Diego's Stuart Collection, for works that are sited on school campuses; and the *NAMES Project AIDS Memorial Quilt*, as an example of grassroots collectivism and social activism. We conclude with a case study comparing two sites in Chicago, the Harold Washington Library Center and Millennium Park, to consider why the former has difficulty securing an engaged audience, while the latter may indeed forecast the direction of public art in the twenty-first century.

The Trouble with (Re)Development

Cities can be intoxicating places, but they can be overwhelming and inhospitable too. Despite Le Corbusier's utopian vision of "a spectacle of order and vitality" (1929: 322), if his 1922 plan for "A Contemporary City for Three Million People" had been built, the streets of Paris would have succumbed to an unrelenting symmetry more imposing than Baron Haussmann's sweeping boulevards of the nineteenth century. Not surprisingly, public art has often been a corrective, particularly in the city, where it functions as an aesthetic band-aid suturing ruptures in the social fabric. Enhancing the visual appeal of public places can go a long way in terms of bolstering community satisfaction and interest but as Malcom Miles noted, public art has been increasingly co-opted to serve private interests, especially real estate development, without sustained critical examination of those projects' effects. He concludes public art's contributions to urban regentrification may indeed be "speculative," especially when the values of art are conceived as "independent of the problems of city life" (1997: 1, 12). By the late 1980s, Patricia Phillips complained public space was only that which had been "left over" by private developers after the real estate boom, lamenting that "the clear delineation of a public space has been packaged as a neighborly gesture, with public art the fence that identifies boundaries" (1988: 93).

In *Evictions: Art and Spatial Politics*, Rosalyn Deutsche utilized "spatial-cultural" discourse to examine the contested terrain of public space, and its growing privatization. She lodged a battery of charges against so-called "redevelopment" schemes (and their manipulations of public art), which supposedly reinvigorate ailing urbanism, but seem to serve mostly well-heeled citizens, tourists, and the developers. Deutsche decries – mostly male – academics who fortify leftist spatial theories at the expense of other philosophies and movements, particularly feminism. In their agendas she identifies a tendency to simplify social spaces as unitary entities, rather than acknowledge their fragmentary nature and shifting socio-political dynamics. Though redevelopment projects are often promoted as socially responsible and collectively produced, Deutsche notes that many of these reinforce socio-economic inequities, and contribute to social problems such as homelessness. By focusing on matters of beauty and utility, Deutsche argues, developers neutralize highly charged issues of class and race that shape public space. She concludes that redevelopment projects and public art are called upon to "reify as natural the conditions of the late capitalist city," and thus community, "both as territory and social form," is undermined by profit-motivated developers and short-sighted politicians. Deutsche's warnings can feel a bit one-sided, especially when considering some of the benefits the private sector might bring to public art (see Chapter 4). Yet even well-intentioned builders, ignorant of the economic and cultural history of a place earmarked for redevelopment, can actually further entrench social strata. Deutsche correctly asserts that those who myopically focus upon aesthetics and technical issues of production lose sight of the socio-political forces determining the evolution and shifting uses of a place. Developers who provide basic amenities and claim to beautify places on everyone's behalf try to cast their efforts in a moralistic light, which

smoothes over cultural differences, and the realities of disenfran-
chisement and displacement that can accompany gentrification.
Simply making beautiful spaces is not enough; developers must
thoughtfully consider their social functions (1992: 158–61, 164–8;
1996). Otherwise, as John Hannigan fears, private spaces will continue to replace public ones, creating a solipsistic "city of illusion,"
physically, economically, and culturally isolated from, and impervious to, its neighbors and their concerns (1998: 2–11). Michael
Sorkin condemns "urban renewal with a sinister twist"; a proliferation of insulated borders, increased surveillance and segregation,
and pastiche in place of historical styles (1992: xiv–xv). Of course,
such trends are not confined to the city; our suburban sprawl generates many opportunistic development schemes – witness the growth
of "privatopias," cul-de-sacs bursting at the seams with McMansions
(Hayden 2006). What are the historical and cultural costs of a
"gentrification" mindset, which disposes with the past when it
becomes inconvenient or unprofitable? Dolores Hayden laments
that many designers possess only fragmentary knowledge of our
built environment's history, and thus the dazzling schemes they
conceive to rehabilitate places can end up in effect killing them
(Hayden 1992: 262–3).

Many gentrified spaces send mixed signals; they seem public, but
in actuality are private endeavors whose communal spaces are included
to meet zoning requirements and present their developers as
civic-spirited. For Deutsche, Battery Park City (BPC) is a troubling
example of such gentrification. BPC is a multi-billion-dollar redevelopment project, sited on 92 acres of landfill along the waterfront of
New York's Lower West Side. Under the behest of the New York
State legislature, the BPC Authority (a "public benefit" corporation)
was created in 1968. The Authority develops BPC's public spaces,
and coordinates the efforts of private developers who lease the land,
making sure they adhere to design guidelines emphasizing environmental consciousness. Though low- and moderate-income housing
were part of its initial conception, by the time BPC was built in the
1980s these objectives were pushed aside (Wiley 1991: 270, 273).
Contrary to the fact that many of its artworks are "totally accessible
to the public" (Marter 1989: 318), Deutsche finds BPC ultimately
exclusionary; mostly high-end housing and commercial businesses,

buffered by politically correct public spaces. Martha Rosler concurs, characterizing BPC as an "urban fortress" where public spaces screen "enclaves of wealth" (1991: 17, 32). M. Christine Boyer is also critical of BPC, complaining that its "recycled architectural elements and styles borrowed from the city's best residential sections" were used to justify "the expenditure of public money in an essentially private domain" (1992: 194–5). Undoubtedly, BPC's developers wished to turn a profit, but one could also argue that they tried to create vibrant public spaces. Since its reconception in 1979, the BPC proposal included art. Much of what followed at BPC either blends in with the environment, or dutifully regurgitates public art's now-popular conventions (for example, Stuart Crawford's *Police Memorial* on BPC's Esplanade is quite derivative of Lin's *Vietnam Veterans Memorial*; see Chapter 2). Yet people do feel comfortable interacting with the art here, and some of it ventures social commentary. Tom Otterness' *The Real World* (1992) is a sculptural playground where a Lilliputian civilization of bronze figures (seemingly lifted from Bosch's *Garden of Earthly Delights*) cavorts, chasing after a trail of coins while a "fat cat" presides over the scene. The work reads as a cautionary "allegory of greed," with the financial district looming nearby (Brenson 1996: 33; Senie 2003: 195–6). Overall BPC is a pleasant place, but it feels like a quality-controlled, sanitized model of New York, rather than part of the city. It is decidedly upscale, offering spectacular views of the river from its magnificent public spaces, though these seem to be used mostly by neighborhood residents. The subtext here is that beauty, quiet, cleanliness, and safety come at the exclusion of lower- and middle-income housing. Our behaviors here are also closely managed, as most clearly evidenced by the proliferation of signage throughout BPC. We are reminded not to feed squirrels and pigeons; skateboarders and bikers are told to "respect others, go slow"; and dogs are encouraged not to bark, with help from their owners who can translate the "shhh" sign at the dog run. All visitors to BPC are implored to "Please be courteous. Let's work together for a better community."

Some artists use biting irony to challenge developers' assertions that gentrification is good for all of us. Rachel Whiteread's *House* (1993–4, sponsored by Artangel) was a concrete cast of a Victorian row home, slated for demolition in a governmental "improvement" plan for a working-class neighborhood in London's East End. The cast was so arresting that it demanded immediate attention, and lingered in the mind as a ghostly vestige long after the sculpture was destroyed just three months after its creation, against the artist's wishes (Freedman 2004: 238). Krzysztof Wodiczko's works, which effectively "augment individual autonomy and make visible certain forms of social oppression," are equally evocative (Thompson and Sholette 2004: 19). Wodiczko sees his work as "critical public art," making "aesthetic-critical interruptions, infiltrations and appropriations that question the symbolic, psychopolitical and economic operations of the city" (1987: 42). The artist is best known for his slide projection pieces, such as those done in New York's Union Square Park during its regentrification in the 1980s. Onto the park's freshly restored nineteenth-century monuments, Wodiczko projected images of homeless people, one of the populations forced out of the area by such redevelopment and historic preservation efforts. Thus he made the monuments witnesses "to the sociospatial conflicts that they were being employed to conceal" (Deutsche 1996: xv), and the projections "counter-monuments" that both "revive" and "disturb" their original sources (Kaye 2000: 33–5, 38). Wodiczko's *Homeless Vehicle Project* (1988) was a response to Mayor Ed Koch's 1987 mandate that all homeless persons in New York undergo psychiatric evaluations, which could force them to be hospitalized. Designed in consultation with his "co-artists" (Thompson and Sholette 2004: 19, 27–8), in this case members of the city's homeless population, the *Homeless Vehicle Project* provided mobile shelter, a can and bottle collection facility, and storage. Intended not as a substitute for "permanent, safe, and dignified shelter" but as advocacy for such, the project addressed immediate survival needs while exposing the deeply troubling socio-economic realities that compelled "fellow urban citizens" to live on the streets. Thus Wodiczko would not allow us to ignore the homeless "as identity-free objects that must be negotiated rather than recognized," nor regentrification's part in the creation of that population and its plight (Lurie and Wodiczko 1988: 54–5, 58). The attendant costs and dangers of redevelopment are causes for genuine concern, but I would argue are best served by such powerful ruminations on life in the wake of regentrification's path, instead of alarmist anti-capitalist rhetoric.

——————— **Nonprofits and the Ephemeral Idyll** ———————

Historically nonprofit organizations have been effective means through which to harness private energies for public good. Often they are held up as the primary, if not the sole, example of private interests at work in public art, usually to the exclusion of for-profit businesses. My purpose in addressing nonprofits in this last chapter is to underscore their vital role, while affording the commercial entities examined in Chapter 4 the attention that has normally eluded them in the public art canon. According to Jill Medvedow, director of Boston's Institute of Contemporary Art (see Chapter 3), the efficacy of nonprofit organizations resides in their ability to intersect with "other cultural disciplines and diverse communities" to be truly "democratic in their access and availability" (2004: 10). Nonprofits can enter into partnerships with others that extend their reach, coffers, and spheres of influence. In such mutually beneficial relationships, for example, a nonprofit gains legitimacy and clout by aligning forces with a government agency, while an over-stretched municipality is revitalized by an influx of energy from a public-minded private sector. In an age when vision is unlimited but funds are tight, such public–private partnerships may be among the most feasible ways to commission, maintain, and restore works of public art. These partnerships often emphasize advocacy and community involvement, especially at the essential planning phases of a project.

From 1978 to 1985 the Cambridge Arts Council (CAC), a for-public nonprofit, teamed up with the Massachusetts Bay Transportation Authority (MBTA) to develop the "Arts on the Line" program for the Boston subway system's Red Line, then adding new stations. The CAC administered the program, whose funds were provided by the US Department of Transportation through the MBTA. Arts on the Line endeavored to be democratic and open itself to public scrutiny, while still commissioning high-quality, permanent, site-specific works. As such, it became a model for other cities. Art professionals (including those from the respective neighborhoods) selected the artworks, but input was invited from local community members (some of whom served on advisory committees), not only to gain their support, but to better understand the character and social context of each place. "Site bios" detailed the history and demographics of a neighborhood as well as the architecture of the stations, acknowledging the identity shifts that occur between different subway patrons and pockets of the city. Artists, including many from Massachusetts, were brought into the process at the early stages ("Arts on the Line" 1988: 69–70). In the case of Mags Harries' *Glove Cycle* (1978–84) for the new Porter Square station, the artist eventually became and remains a resident of the neighborhood. She rode the subway regularly and began to carefully watch her fellow commuters, thinking about ways to engage without pandering to them. During a particularly harsh winter in 1978 the artist began collecting the many orphaned gloves she found, casting these in bronze (due to budgetary constraints the project was scaled down, so there are fewer gloves than originally intended). These were then scattered throughout the station; along the exceedingly deep escalator, stranded alone, heaped together in a poignant pile. Their placement echoes "the movement pattern of the commuters" through the station, descending to the platforms where they will stand isolated or in clusters waiting for the train (Fleming and von Tscharner 1981: 110). Harries describes the piece as a sort of life-cycle, which works nicely given the anthropomorphic nature of the gloves. (The first gloves encountered at the top of the escalator are that of a child inside another one belonging to a woman; the cycle ends with a pile that looks like a glove graveyard.) The project offers station users a sense of discovery; there are playful interjections, such as two gloves embedded in the floor, reenacting Michelangelo's famed *Creation of Adam* scene from the Sistine Chapel ceiling. The *Glove Cycle* has clearly become entrenched in the public's consciousness; the artist notes that it is still mentioned to her nearly every day, and people even call to report when the gloves require cleaning. In fact, when architects worried the piece would detract from the station's "formal, clean aesthetic," it was the neighborhood residents who fought for it. Though it is quite different from her work now, Harries maintains great affection for the *Glove Cycle* (Harries 2006), which is fortunate since she sees it several times daily as she travels to and from home.

Two of the most celebrated and enduring public art nonprofits are Creative Time, Inc., and the Public Art Fund, Inc. Each is based in New York City, was founded in the 1970s, and unlike Arts on the Line focuses on temporary works. By utilizing supposedly non-art public venues, these nonprofits "de-ghettoize" art (Dubin 1992: 264), challenging the physical and social parameters of both art and its audiences. Creative Time is probably still best known for *Art on the Beach* (first held in 1978), an annual, outdoor seasonal event showcasing collaborative projects, whose structure changed each year. The Public Art Fund (PAF) seeks to make contemporary art "understood and appreciated by the widest possible audience" (Freedman 2004: 7). Its *Messages to the Public*, a decade-long series started in 1982, featured a different artist's 20- to 30-second "spot" each month, which played about 50 times daily on Times Square's massive Spectacolor lightboard (since replaced by the Panasonic Astrovision screen). Participants included Jenny Holzer, Edgar-Heap-of-Birds, and Barbara Kruger. What ensued was unexpected and sometimes uncomfortable commentary on the friction between consumption and art. Messages such as Martha Rosler's *Housing is a Human Right* (1989) flashed amid the rapid flicker of commercial advertisements, providing "unregulated encounters" with art for a largely "unprepared" potential audience of nearly one and a half million people each day (Miles 1989: 30–1; Phillips 1992: 300–1).

More recent projects under the PAF's "In the Public Realm" program display equal amounts of substance and provocation. Christine Hill's *Tourguide?* (1999) was an extended performance piece, in which the artist took paying customers on "highly person-alized" walking tours of SoHo as a means of cultivating randomness while interrogating "interpersonal commerce." There was also Jeff Koon's iconic *Puppy*, restaged in Rockefeller Center in the summer of 2000. This 43-foot-tall sculpture of a West Highland terrier was constructed of an armature that provided internal irrigation for over 70,000 flowering plants. *Puppy* managed to be unapologeti-cally kitschy and cute, while maintaining a "strategically ambiguous stance toward consumer culture." And Lawrence Weiner's *New York City Manhole Covers* (2000) consisted of 19 such covers in various locations on the streets of Lower Manhattan. Though these were fully functional they also sported an enigmatic text, "IN DIRECT LINE WITH ANOTHER & THE NEXT," which referenced the city's grid plan and "the myriad physical and personal relationships that are constantly reformulated within that grid" (Freedman 2004: 112, 129, 231). The PAF projects are quintessentially populist; their content and forms are comprehensible to wide and varied audiences, but meaning is open-ended enough to invite all kinds of interpretations.

That many such populist-minded efforts have resulted in temporary artworks is significant. Yet for many artists and arts administrators, the success of public art initiatives is calculated by the ability to place works permanently. On one hand this makes sense; permanency confers status, indicating that a work is so good it deserves to be seen and preserved for generations. But a myopic emphasis on permanency tends to favor physical access and widespread appeal above all other aspects of public art, seeking universally "timeless" themes (Apgar 1992: 24). Phillips cautions us that such "naively constructed prescriptions ... based on information and impressions formed more than a century ago" can be dangerous to public art's health. Permanent works like a traditional equestrian portrait in a park can be so fully absorbed into their settings and so familiar to us that they go unnoticed, becoming "amiable bronze Pop art" invisible to our eyes and unconsidered by our hearts and minds (Heartney and Gopnik 2005: 9). Such works are also prone to play things too safely, trying to sidestep controversy by avoiding any offenses now or in the future. In contrast, Phillips argues, temporary works can be "maverick" and "focused" without having to give up their resonant qualities (1988: 94–6; 1992: 303). Permanent works are more likely to have difficulty gaining support, and must renegotiate their relationships with changing publics over time. But a permanent project is not necessarily more public than a temporary and timely one.

As we have already seen with *The Gates* (Chapters 2 and 4), temporary works can deftly grab and maintain the public's attention with their "Hurry, hurry see them now before they disappear!" urgency. Garry Apgar's preference for permanency led him to describe Christo and Jeanne-Claude's works as "provocative and often witty projects" that "are not public art ... but highly personal critiques ... about the notion of art in public places." But he also acknowledges "nothing lasts forever," defining "permanent" as "likely to last for generations ... as an enduring bond" (1992: 27, 29, n. 12).

140

Thus even by Apgar's time-based standards, Christo and Jeanne-Claude are public artists. They undertake lengthy, even decades-long, projects; address complex logistical concerns; and realize works that have sustaining impact beyond their few weeks of physical installation. Their artworks are process-oriented events, not self-contained objects. Many aspects of these events are carefully choreographed: the "protracted courtship" of landowners, local citizens, and government officials, from whom the artists need approval; their exhaustive surveying of sites and environmental impact studies; the ritual-like movements of workers who install the pieces; and the photographic and video/film documentation of the processes as they unfold (van der Marck 1992: 102–5). Ultimately their works "measure the distance between art's aspirations and society's permissions," functioning as "gigantic parables; subversive, beautiful, didactic" (O'Doherty 1981: 338). The ephemeral nature of Christo and Jeanne-Claude's projects is essential to their efficacy. They prompt no concern that an undesirable neighbor is being foisted upon the public for all time; rather, their work offers a temporary interjection into a given environment, makes its statement, and then moves on and out. If their schemes were intended to be permanent it is highly unlikely that any of them would ever be actualized, both on conceptual and logistical bases. But because their works are temporary, Christo and Jeanne-Claude can take big risks, though of course their projects are never really gone. While the physical objects may be dismantled after a few weeks, the art lives on through extensive visual documentation, and more importantly, through the memories of those who have seen it. In this way, Christo and Jeanne-Claude's works become the mental property of anyone who has experienced them, a thoroughly populist notion.

Certainly permanent and temporary public artworks ought to be encouraged to coexist with and reinforce one another. But in his study of postmodernism's effects on culture, David Harvey pointed out an essential irony inherent in "aesthetic theory": it seeks to convey "eternal and immutable truths" always "in the midst of the maelstrom of flux and change" (1980: 205). A recurrent problem for permanent, site-specific art is its difficulty in maintaining "appropriateness to the site," which may be drastically transformed since the artist first addressed it (Senie 1992b: 230). But while permanent art has trouble

141

responding to changes in environment, aesthetic tastes, cultural values, or audience, the more experimental nature of temporary works can accommodate such shifts, without having to impose a coherent constituency where none can be claimed. Impermanent works can circumvent logistical challenges such as long-term maintenance and upkeep, persistent vandalism, and physical wear. Artists can also tackle timely, hot-button topics, and more easily quell controversy and censorship when audiences are assured that the art is "just visiting." As Phillips insists, "the temporary in public art is not about an absence of commitment or involvement, but about an intensification and enrichment of the conception of public" (1992: 304).

Back to School

In some respects – not all being very fortunate – a university is like a business, which must secure its future through its finances. Thus like corporations seeking to raise their profiles and improve public relations, colleges can utilize art as a sort of marketing tool. But institutions of learning are uniquely positioned to offer art a context that most corporations cannot; instead of selling you products, they proffer education through a "tradition of open inquiry" (Beardsley 1981a: 55). Not every college has art, let alone a visionary plan for its acquisition or the funds to collect it. But those universities with art on their campuses have a great advantage over many other public art venues; their potential audiences are more likely to be receptive to any of the art's attendant didactic agendas. One can safely presume that most of the people (students, faculty, staff, board members, and others) who come on campus to partake of its events and facilities have a friendly predisposition toward the school's educational mission. They may not choose to pursue the art any further than taking note of it as a convenient landmark on campus, but if they become genuinely interested in it there are usually ample resources on-site to learn more. As discussed in Chapter 3, despite their best efforts many art museums are still branded as elitist institutions, having little to do with daily life. While Ivy League schools remain the benchmarks of academic prestige, more Americans are going to college than ever before, dispelling the myth that higher education is reserved only for the wealthiest and most privileged. In fact, the proliferation of state schools and community colleges bespeaks a particularly populist notion; that an education should be available and affordable to anyone who wants it. And in rural or other communities where access to the arts might be limited, a university often becomes the primary cultural resource.

Even when they are private, most educational institutions permit at least some public use of their facilities. Of course, some universities deliberately or subconsciously discourage this, fortifying their borders with gates and walls, or isolating their campuses in remote locales. But even when access is limited, the public is usually able and sometimes even invited to visit, free of charge. This is quite different from museums, where admission fees are standard, and the agendas are art-specific. In contrast, most colleges and universities (other than institutions dedicated to the study of a particular field) are places where an incredibly vast range of interests are pursued, art being only one of them. The diversity of a college setting can alleviate pressure from our encounters with the art found there: we are not expected to be art experts or even enthusiasts, though we may choose to become such; and art is not the sole beacon of enlightenment, but one component in a more comprehensive education. This situation makes universities ideal hosts for art; their multiple facilities are ready stage-sets for indoor and outdoor, as well as permanent and temporary, artworks of all kinds. With the subsequent renovations and additions most campuses undergo come opportunities to expand a collection, reconfigure the art, or create site-specific projects. Since colleges gather a heterogeneous group of specialists, spaces, and disciplines at a shared location, their art can address numerous subjects that reflect rather than limit the range of audiences, and explore the depth of collective bodies of knowledge instead of collapsing them. Today many schools are more aware of and exploring their abilities to amiably host public art. For example, in 2006 the art departments of Hamilton College and Colgate University jointly sponsored "Public Art on Campus," a symposium with artist Mary Miss as the featured speaker, which envisioned a strong future for public art and proactive roles for public artists on college campuses.

In Chapter 2 we encountered some art initiatives at MIT; here we consider the University of California at San Diego's campus in La Jolla (UCSD), which hosts the Stuart Collection. UCSD, established in 1962, occupies a gorgeous site overlooking the Pacific Ocean. Though renowned for work in the sciences, the institution also has a formidable art program with a succession of art stars serving as faculty. In 1981 local businessman James Stuart DeSilva struck a "collaborative agreement" with UCSD: the school would serve as the site for an art collection; and his Stuart Foundation, a private organization, would foot the bills. (Since then additional funding from various sources, including the NEA, has also been obtained.) With the added support of the university chancellor, the Stuart Collection bypassed "many of the bureaucratic obstacles that often limit collections of public sculpture." David Joselit is particularly impressed by how its artworks are integrated so "effectively into the fabric of campus life" that "it is not unusual to encounter them without warning" (1989: 131–2). Conceived to embody a diversity of techniques and tastes, the Stuart Collection transcends its benefactor's individual preferences. The collection does not attempt to be all things to all people or represent every form of public art, but focuses on outdoor sculpture that either bears a direct relationship to its respective site, or offers commentary on campus activities. Alexis Smith's *Snake Path* (1989–92) provides a cautionary narrative on the institutional and personal accountability that comes with education. Here pedestrians hike a 560-foot-long, 10-foot-wide trail that ambles uphill to the Central Library. Paving stones replicate the pattern of a snake's skin, with the snake's tail at the hill's base and its forked tongue stretching toward the library's entrance at the summit. As the path winds through its course, it passes a monumental stone book inscribed with a passage from John Milton's *Paradise Lost*, and encloses a small circular garden meant to evoke Eden. Joselit suggests such references recall "the biblical conflict between innocence and knowledge" and remind one of "the ethical responsibilities of knowledge – a particularly important issue at a university so deeply involved in scientific research." *Snake Path* is both a witty acknowledgement of tensions between the school's agendas and obligations, and a functional amenity providing passage to an important research facility. As the physical repository and symbolic seat of information amassed at the institution, the library site surely inspired Smith's meditation on the acquisition of wisdom. The Stuart Collection is not an assembly of "isolated trophies" (Joselit 1989: 133–4), but a compilation of unique critical responses to the university. Though each artwork could stand on its own as a discrete entity, together the collection forges a more cohesive visual identity and conceptual framework for a diverse and rambling campus. As such it offers a viable model for public art with populist aspirations, which could certainly extend beyond the schoolyard.

Grieving Loss, Remembering Life

Memorials remain one of the longest-standing traditions in public art, though their appearance has often changed. Despite the current military and political tensions around the globe, a bronze portrait of a war hero seems out of step with contemporary culture. But the *NAMES Project AIDS Memorial Quilt* is timely and evocative. Begun in San Francisco in 1987 under the aegis of activist Cleve Jones, the *Quilt* was a grassroots response to the AIDS crisis, then negligently ignored by the American government, still mysterious to the medical community, and embattled by social discrimination (Dubin 1992: 198). Jones traces the impetus for the *Quilt* to a candlelight procession for George Moscone and Harvey Milk he attended in 1985, at which he asked people to write names of those who died of AIDS on placards. To "stunning effect" these were affixed to the façade of a federal building, creating "a wall of memory that, simply by naming names, exposed both private loss and public indifference" (Hawkins 1993: 756). By late February of 1987 Jones made the first panel of the *Quilt* for his best friend, Marvin Feldman. The NAMES Project was officially launched in June of that year, and the *Quilt*, already having about 2,000 panels, made its first public appearance in October at the National March on Washington for Lesbian and Gay Rights. Today there are 91,000 individuals memorialized in the *Quilt*, attesting to the scope of the AIDS tragedy and our need to remember. The *Quilt* has become an international phenomenon, with other countries creating their own versions. It has also inspired other AIDS-related art projects including the *National AIDS Memorial Grove* (established 1989), a garden for contemplation and bereavement, sited in a formerly neglected section of San Francisco's Golden Gate Park.

The *NAMES Quilt* is both an individual and a communal endeavor. As Peter Hawkins suggests, to some degree it operates beyond the will of the dead; it is the survivors who decide that it is meaningful to place the deceased "in the context (and company) of the AIDS epidemic" (1993: 778). People make panels for loved ones – or someone they may not have ever met – lost to AIDS, an activity bringing together "normally opposite feelings" like "grief and pride-in-work" (Weinstein 1989: 48). Each panel is a 6-by-3-foot swath of fabric, approximating the size of a coffin, which is subsequently joined to a block of 31 other panels from the same geographical region. Though Jones is not an artist, his conception of the *Quilt* drew upon art-specific precedents, particularly the collaborative efforts and pointed political statements of feminist artists such as Judy Chicago. Jones was also inspired by Christo and Jeanne-Claude, not only for their use of fabric, but for their staging of massive, process-oriented works. And of course there is Maya Lin's *Vietnam Veterans Memorial* (see Chapter 2), which demanded that the dead and missing be accounted for, and literally named each of them (Weinstein 1989: 52). Despite these sources, the *Quilt* continues to prompt the query: In order to fully realize social power, must aesthetics be compromised? My answer is a resounding "No" – activism and aesthetics are interdependent here. The *Quilt* shakes us out of complacency and makes visible and specific the losses brought by AIDS. While many of the techniques and styles used to memorialize the dead are not sophisticated, genuine sentiment imbues them with aesthetic as well as emotional force. Bold colors or shiny sequins counter death's dulling effects on the body and memory. Though there are strange juxtapositions in style and mood, cohesion exists. Beyond the expected elements of names and birth and death dates, many panels share unplanned similarities, such as personal items like clothing or teddy bears. This is reminiscent of traditional mourning or memory quilts, which displayed the deceased's name and used his or her clothing to add an "emotional dimension" (Mainardi 1973: 340–1; 1988: 53). The *NAMES Quilt* possesses a disquieting irony; quilting transcends its place in nostalgic American history to bear witness to an epidemic burdened by cultural stigma (Crichton 1992: 292). Patricia Mainardi observes that because of their functionalism and connotations of an "honest" if "romanticized" past, quilts "seem to speak of a better world, and when that is coupled with a politically explicit content, they become icons of moral authority" (1988: 53).

Jones remembered a quilt used in his own family to comfort those who were sick or housebound, and liked its associations of coziness and community. But not only are quilts comforting, they were once artworks common to many American homes that also recorded personal history in the domestic sphere. In the *NAMES Quilt* fabric becomes a metaphor for the fragility of human life (Weinstein 1989: 44; Hawkins 1993: 757, 765–7). Among those remembered, there are no distinctions by social class, race, ethnicity, sexual preference, gender, or age; each person gets the same size panel. Hawkins identifies an "internal pluralism" here. In a way the *Quilt* is "authorless"; beyond the guidelines of size and including the deceased's name, contributors are free to choose their materials and styles. And the *Quilt* attempts no "metanarrative" to tell a "single story" or set a "particular tone," which means no response to it is more appropriate than any other. In fact, the agency of individual viewers is greatly enhanced, as no one tells us "where to start, finish, or pay particular attention" (1993: 763–4, 779).

The *Quilt*'s scale is arresting when spread on the ground, a massive graveyard literally blanketing the earth. It cannot be easily ignored or shrugged off like an "unpleasant" story on the evening news. For its public exhibitions, *Quilt* staffers and volunteers dressed in white ritualistically unfold and arrange the panels with reverence, a mood that is echoed in the slow, purposeful movements of viewers. The enormity of the AIDS crisis is made palpable during these displays as the names of those remembered are read aloud; one could listen for hours and never hear the same name twice. The contrast between the *Quilt*'s seemingly endless sprawl and the intimacy of its human-sized components enlivens it further; just like the epidemic, its scope is vast but its impact is intimate. Though dwarfed by the *Quilt*'s immensity we experience it a unique panel at a time. This serves to make "irreplaceable personal lives" publicly known, and to elevate the story of AIDS beyond detached statistics to "a spectacular demonstration of the feminist dictum, the personal *is* political" (Crichton 1992: 291; Hawkins 1993: 774, 777). Yet the power of the *Quilt* is found not only in its size (some argue that it need get no bigger to make its point), but in the intensity of feelings it generates. The *Quilt*'s collaborators may have never met each other yet share a sense of purpose and tragic loss, perhaps consoling each other with the knowledge that they are not alone as their individual panels amplify and fortify each other. E. G. Crichton links the *Quilt*'s collaborative nature and "craft"-like materials to the feminist art movement, which emphasized (auto)-biographical content and process over finished products, while undermining categorical distinctions between "high" and "low" (1992: 287, 289–92). Since most of the *Quilt*'s makers are not professional artists, they probably approached their contributions as expressions of grief rather than artistic endeavors. Their labors are subsumed into a collective enterprise without any single panel being more significant than another, yet they retain distinctive voices. In outlining the strengths of collaboration, Olivia Gude argued that such a situation is the best possible outcome: individual visions are not absorbed as unrecognizable parts of a whole, but are accumulated as multiple points of view, allowed to coexist and "harmonize" (1989: 323).

Despite the *Quilt*'s potent aesthetics and conviction, the art world still seems unable to adequately deal with it. As Crichton observes; "Unlike most of what we find in galleries and museums, the Quilt has a connection to our daily lives that seems unrelated to the remote world of 'high art,' or 'fine art'." But she also suggests that its power is enhanced by the ability to thrive "outside established art channels"; the *Quilt* was not created by "art stars," cannot be commercially marketed, and earned public recognition without much help from art critics (1992: 287, 289). Mainardi exposes the sexism that relegated quilting to the "feminine" world of "craft" rather than "high" art. She asserts that, historically, quilting actually provided women with opportunities to express themselves creatively and to participate in political discourse (either symbolized in their quilts, or through networking with others at quilting bees). She also notes that quilting was neither anonymous nor always collective, though it is often conceived as such, and that quilts resisted the market economy, being given or used rather than bought or sold. But even though Mainardi argues so eloquently for the quilt's significance as an artform, she still considers that by the NAMES Project primarily as a "political quilt," rather than an "art quilt" (1973: 331–8, 341–2, 344; 1988: 49–53).

One day after we had finished viewing the Academy Award-winning documentary, *Common Threads: Stories from the Quilt* (1989), my introductory art history/appreciation class embarked on a passionate discussion. After some back-and-forth on the question of its "art" status, one of my students said he was uncomfortable with the line of inquiry because the *Quilt* needed to be "above" art concerns as its message is so important. While full immunity from critical reproach is impractical and undesirable, his comment underscores an essential point in the call for a more populist approach to public art; some works are so powerful, so resonant, and matter so much, that they rightfully elevate the public's opinion above that of critics and art professionals. And in these instances instead of bemoaning them, critics and art professionals could take their cues from members of the public. As Jeff Weinstein demonstrates in his 1989 essay on the *Quilt*, "Names Carried into the Future," a first-person narrative (in this case by a gay man) can sometimes be the most effective and appropriate form of criticism. Ultimately, it is probably much less useful to define and ordain works as "art" than to discern their ability to move, disturb, or provoke us. But the *Quilt* is surely public art at its best. It brings attention to a public health crisis; unflinchingly addresses prevailing socio-political concerns; and refuses to engage in niceties, or skirt tough issues with vagaries (Crichton 1992: 289). The *Quilt* meets us during our daily activities (exhibited at places like school gyms and shopping malls); seeks to raise social consciousness; and provides a cathartic experience for its makers. It also explores widely shared experiences of loss while acknowledging the AIDS epidemic's personal dimensions, giving public voice to private mourning.

The *Quilt* was last shown in its entirety in 1996, spread out on Washington's Mall where it received over a million visitors. Since then it has had troubles, fiscal and otherwise. The NAMES Foundation moved to Atlanta in 2001, and its relationship with Jones is irreparably damaged. (A wrongful termination suit brought by Jones resulted in a settlement granting him some of the panels though he has yet to receive these, a dispute that continues at this writing.) Though AIDS remains a persistent tragedy, in the United States and around the world, detractors suggest that the *Quilt* has lost its relevance: its urgency being quieted by new drug treatments that have shifted the focus to living rather than dying with AIDS; and its efficacy undermined by its sentimentality, or that it is too large to be displayed in a single place anymore (McKinley 2007). But as Hawkins contends, the *Quilt*'s achievement was to widen its circle beyond the gay community, to leave "behind ghetto and closet, to bring mourning from the margin to the center" (1993: 760, 762–3, 778). Certainly artworks do not have to exist outside traditional art channels to achieve the appeal and resonance of the *Quilt*, but the art world would be wise to learn from projects that effectively merge social message with artistic expression. Both the *Quilt*'s aesthetic beauty and social power are enhanced by the tragic condition of its existence – an eerie knowledge that it is unfinished.

--------- **Two Tales in One City** ---------

The city of Chicago has a long and vigorous history with public art. Some of its "triumphs" were hard-won, such as that of the so-called *Chicago Picasso*. Privately commissioned in 1965 by Skidmore, Owings and Merrill, which designed the Civic Center where it was placed, the *Chicago Picasso* was not immediately embraced upon its installation in 1967. As an abstract portrait conflating Picasso's wife and dog, constructed of industrial-looking Cor-Ten steel, it required much coaxing before the citizenry warmed up to it, though since it has become a beloved city mascot. We now turn to a comparison of two public art venues in Chicago, the Harold Washington Library Center and Millennium Park, which illuminate the contours of a populist approach to public art. The Washington Library, named after the deceased mayor, is a central branch of the city's public library system. Its art collection was initiated in the late 1980s as part of a municipal percent-for-art program, with the intention of obtaining high-quality works while challenging "conventional institutional prescriptions of public art." The collection emphasizes local contemporary artists, and strives to represent the city's diverse population; community representatives served on its advisory panel, and the Alliance for Cultural Equity pushed Chicago's Department of Cultural Affairs to guarantee "significant minority representation" (Dubin 1992: 66). Despite a concerted effort to be culturally sensitive, the collection still has its critics who complain that it is neither diverse nor inclusive enough, and that it was shaped too much by aesthetic rather than social criteria (Snodgrass 1992: 18, 21–3).

Art in the Washington Library is of varied quality, and at times relates only minimally to the architectural setting or library context. Works by Nancy Spero, Alison Saar, Jacob Lawrence, Edgar-Heap-of-Birds, and the Chicago Imagists Ed Pashke and Roger Brown are exhibited alongside those by lesser-known artists. Some of the collection's best works are in remote or limited access places such as *Amerika – For the Authors of Chicago* (1991). This series of 32 collaborative images was inspired by Franz Kafka's unfinished novel, and made by Tim Rollins and Kids of Survival (KOS). The Rollins/KOS collaboration began in the early 1980s; as a participant in New York's "Learning to Read Through the Arts" program, Rollins worked with "remedial" students in the South Bronx. Initially dismayed over book defacement, Rollins commenced a series of cooperative art projects in which students make visual responses to classic works of literature read aloud, usually painting or drawing on pages of text, which are then collectively edited. Some critics questioned Rollins' motivations as the collaboration was nearly an overnight success in the art world. But it is hard to deny that the students, many of whom had been written off as academically challenged or socially troubled, were empowered to have their intellectual and artistic capabilities recognized (Rosser 1989: 127–32; Lippard 1990: 169). For *Amerika* Rollins collaborated with Chicago public high school students, who created works on pages of text either about Chicago or by Chicago authors. The series is hung in the Chicago Authors Meeting Room and although well suited to the space, the glass-wall partitions make this seem inaccessible, effectively segregating it from the rest of the library. When I visited on a busy

Saturday, the room went totally unused. It would also be easy to miss Joseph Kosuth's *A Play: News from Kafka and a Quote* (1991), which juxtaposes text from various authors, quotes from Kafka's *Parables*, and a *Washington Post* article on the public's feelings of political powerlessness. But despite its advocacy for public agency, the siting of Kosuth's piece in the extravagant Winter Garden's foyer is unwelcoming. The Garden is usually reserved for private functions, and security personnel are used to keep the public at bay during such events. Were Kosuth's work sited on the ground floor, encountered when patrons first enter, it could provide a conceptual foundation upon which to build the library visit, a tangible connection between art and the quest for knowledge.

A library disseminates information to its public, and thus can offer a rich context for art. But ultimately the Washington Library collection seems stagnant, and while the art does not disappear into its surroundings, it does not distinguish itself enough either. Amid the building's handsome furnishings and architectural details, much of the art comes across as decoration rather than social commentary. The collection has received scant attention from critics since its unveiling in 1991, and seems to garner little more from library patrons. The best of intentions may not be able to save the collection from one of the most corrosive threats to public art – audience disinterest.

Comparatively, Chicago's Millennium Park is a veritable seat of populism. One has to wonder if the setting, park as opposed to library, may partially account for this difference. Sitting outdoors on a beautiful day obviously offers charms with which even the best libraries, however well appointed, cannot compete. But clearly there is more afoot here, and the "successes" of Millennium Park deserve further discussion. The park, a 475-million-dollar project sited on 24.5 acres of prime real estate, opened in July 2004. It was conceived in the late 1990s under Mayor Richard M. Daley's administration as a public–private collaboration to rehabilitate the blighted site of a former rail yard. The city paid for the park's foundation and infrastructure, while private donations were raised to fund art and architecture "enhancements." This nomenclature is misleading as it implies these are decorative afterthoughts, when in fact the works of Gehry, Plensa, and Kapoor constitute the heart of the park.

The *Pritzker Pavilion*, designed by Frank O. Gehry, is a state-of-the-art outdoor music facility with an acoustical canopy, for which the adjacent *BP Bridge* (also by Gehry) acts as a sound barrier to nearby traffic. But not all of the park's "enhancements" work so well. The complex narrative of the *Lurie Garden*, symbolizing Chicago's past and future, is so inscrutable that without any explanation it is surely lost on most visitors. The *Boeing Galleries*, while admirable in their intention to offer art outdoor exhibit spaces (www.millenniumpark.org), are really just sidewalks with armatures upon which to hang placards. And *Wrigley Square* with its *Millennium Park Monument*, which re-creates the peristyle colonnade that stood in the same location from 1917 to 1953, is a virtual ghost town compared to the rest of the park.

Millennium Park does not isolate art from other daily functions; in fact its most popular artworks front busy Michigan Avenue, nearby the park's shop, restaurant, and ice rink (during the warm months this is a café and bar). Though moments of quiet contemplation in museum settings are most worthwhile, there is vitality to such mixed-use places often lacking in art-only venues. Without forsaking their "high art" status, Anish Kapoor's *Cloud Gate* and Jaume Plensa's *Crown Fountain* (both 2004) demystify art in a way their neighbor, the Art Institute, is less likely to do. Conceived as a "tribute to Chicagoans," the *Crown Fountain* consists of two 50-foot-tall glass block towers situated in a shallow wading pool. The towers are actually LED screens, projecting the faces of 1,000 different Chicagoans, meant to represent a broad cross-section of the citizenry. Their images were captured by students at the School of the Art Institute who worked with the city's Department of Cultural Affairs to help identify potential subjects. This bank of images is planned to expand over the years, so that it may "reflect the social evolution of the city" (City of Chicago 2005: 31). The faces are shown on an enormous scale, one at a time, rotating randomly every four to five minutes. Since these countenances are not still photographs, but videos recording subtle movements, it often seems as if the projected faces are having silent conversations. Although the water cannot be turned on during the harsh winter months, the videos are projected day and night, year-round. The area around *Crown Fountain* is a lively place: children play in the pool; sheets of water cascade from above with every face change, dousing anyone immediately below; those seated nearby can feel the fountain's spray. The towers are equipped with spigots periodically spouting water, which are lined up with the projected mouths so that the faces act as contemporary gargoyles for the digital age. Every time the spigots spew, the swarms of people who inevitably gather around the fountain gasp and giggle with delight. The *Crown Fountain*'s good humor inspires a convivial environment; amid the pleasant sound of rushing water a sense of community is refreshed.

Cloud Gate, perched on SBC Plaza (formerly the AT&T Plaza), is Kapoor's first public work in this country (Fig. 5). It is also one of the largest outdoor sculptures in the world (110 tons, 66 feet long, and 33 feet high), and yet no one seems overwhelmed by it. Having earned the nickname of "The Bean" for its elliptical contours, *Cloud Gate* was inspired by liquid mercury. Its 168 stainless steel plates were laboriously polished to yield a seamless form, which acts like a funhouse mirror for viewers, whom Kapoor conceived as active "participants" in the work (www.millenniumpark.org). *Cloud Gate* reflects the city's fabled skyline, the sky, and interactions of the public, who crowd around it. People take pictures, laugh at their distorted reflections, "enter" under its 12-foot arch and lie on the ground to marvel at the view, and spend considerable time with the art while repeatedly *touching* it. Perhaps *Cloud Gate*'s only shortcoming is that it receives so many fingerprints, one is reminded of a refrigerator in need of cleaning.

Millennium Park was the first cultural destination in the US to offer a free downloadable audio tour, with commentary from the mayor and some of the park's artists and architects. The tour is intended to make one's experience more "dynamic," using random access technology so that listeners can peruse at their own pace, choosing which portions of the tour, in which order, they would like to hear (cityofchicago.org 2006). There are also maps (which mark audio tour stops) and numerous full-color guides available free at the park's welcome center, as well as knowledgeable park employees throughout (including greeters who give live tours). The park representative I meet proudly notes that Millennium Park is now the US's second most popular tourist destination, the first being Las Vegas' Strip. A look around the park confirms its

Figure 5 Anish Kapoor. *Cloud Gate.* 2004. Millennium Park, Chicago. Photographer: Brooke A. Knight. Courtesy the artist and Gladstone Gallery, New York.

popularity. Millennium Park is a welcoming place to which many people, both Chicagoans and tourists, happily gravitate. Crowds gather, day and night, seeking each other's company in a revitalized public space. Many of the events (concerts, classes, exhibitions) are free; the entire park is accessible for those with disabilities; there is seating throughout; and the art is not treated as too precious. Instead of maintaining an art-exclusive domain, Millennium Park provides lively, resonant art experiences amid daily life activities for large and varied audiences. And these occur without sacrificing the artists' aesthetics or theoretical interests. Might this be a model of the town square for our new millennium?

On an unseasonably warm October afternoon, the park is packed with visitors. Sitting outside at the bar among crowds lunching, watching football on televisions, and regularly interacting with the art, it becomes clear that Millennium Park has gotten something right. The park does have the undeniable imprint of corporate America: its pristine, manicured spaces can seem sterile; security personnel in yellow parkas are a constant presence; and Muzak blares from speakers. "Naming opportunities" proliferate as nearly every part of the park has acquired a sponsor (this sidewalk brought to you by Chase!). No loitering, dogs, or bicycles are allowed. In short, it is an environment with its rules and restrictions, which implores visitors to help maintain its "excellent condition." Yet no apologies are made for the private sector's role. Rather private and public interests have merged to foster a genuinely public space, and build a collection of art for the citizens of Chicago. While all of Millennium Park's elements may never resolve into a fully integrated space, the individual artworks are so engaging they more than make up for the park's deficiencies. At the *Crown Fountain* and *Cloud Gate* touch is no longer a transgressive act, an illicit caress of the otherwise unapproachable, but is openly invited by both works. These pieces are not merely "playful," but encourage actual play. In its few short years Kapoor's *Cloud Gate* has replaced the *Chicago Picasso* as the city's mascot. It appears everywhere, from T-shirts to beer posters. Initially this might be surprising: Kapoor's work is quite abstract, and seems to be descended from more aloof modernist traditions. Though at first it may look suspiciously like plop art, *Cloud Gate* is everything plop art was not: engaging, friendly, accessible, perspective-shifting, concerned with its environment and for its audiences, and oh yes, fun. It certainly seems as if "The Bean" has started a good conversation, and is speaking most people's language.

Throughout this book we have encountered numerous artworks imbued with a populist spirit, ranging from war memorials and street furniture to temporary installations and radical interventions at museums. For dynamic exchanges to persist between artists, audience members, administrators, and museum professionals, all must commit to having open, honest, and ongoing dialogues. When individual voices, not just the monolithic choruses of "art world" or "the people," are heard and respected, art is at its most public.

Bibliography

Adcock, Craig. (1983). "The Big Bad: A Critical Comparison of Mount Rushmore and Modern Earthworks." *Arts Magazine* 57.8 (Apr.): 104–7.

Adcock, Craig. (1990). "Earthworks in the American Desert." *Tema Celeste* 27–28 (Nov.–Dec.): 44–7.

Allen, Jerry. (1985). "How Art Becomes Public." *Going Public: A Field Guide to Developments in Art in Public Places.* Jeffrey L. Cruikshank (ed.). Amherst: Arts Extension Service/Visual Arts Program of the National Endowment for the Arts, 1988. 244–51.

Alloway, Lawrence. (1976). "Site Inspection." *Artforum* 15.2 (Oct.): 49–55.

Alloway, Lawrence. (1996). "The Great Curatorial Dim-Out." *Thinking About Exhibitions.* Reesa Greenberg, Bruce W. Ferguson, and Sandy Nairne (eds.). London: Routledge. 221–30.

Apgar, Garry. (1992). "Redrawing the Boundaries of Public Art." *Sculpture* 11.3 (May–June): 24–9.

Arian, Edward. (1989). *The Unfulfilled Promise: Public Subsidy of the Arts in America.* Philadelphia: Temple University Press.

Arning, Bill, Chin, Mel, Jacob, Wendy, and Kwon, Miwon. (2006). "No Longer 'New': Public Art of the 1980s and 90s in Retrospect." Panel discussion at the List Center for Visual Arts, Massachusetts Institute of Technology, 17 Mar.

(2004). "Art Mobs to Remix MoMA (With Your Help)." Art Mobs official website. http://mod.blogs.com/art_mobs/. Accessed 5 Feb. 2007.

"Arts on the Line: A Case Study in Artist Selection." (1988). *Going Public: A Field Guide to Developments in Art in Public Places.* Jeffrey L. Cruikshank (ed.). Amherst: Arts Extension Service/Visual Arts Program of the National Endowment for the Arts. 69–70.

Ashford, Doug, Ewald, Wendy, Felshin, Nina, and Phillips, Patricia C. (2006). "A Conversation on Social Collaboration." *Art Journal* 65.2 (Summer): 59–82.

Bach, Penny Balkin. (1988). "Choreography and Caution: The Organization of a Conservation Program." *Going Public: A Field Guide to Developments in Art in Public Places.* Jeffrey L. Cruikshank (ed.). Amherst: Arts Extension Service/ Visual Arts Program of the National Endowment for the Arts. 262–76.

Bach, Penny Balkin (ed.). (2001). *New-Land-Marks: Public Art, Community, and the Meaning of Place.* Washington, DC: Editions Ariel/Philadelphia: Fairmount Park Art Association.

Baigell, Matthew. (1989). "A Ramble around Early Earth Works." *Art Criticism* 5.3: 1–15.

Baker, Elizabeth C. (1976). "Artworks on the Land." *Art in the Land: A Critical Anthology of Environmental Art.* Alan Sonfist (ed.). New York: Dutton, 1983. 73–84.

Balfe, Judith H., and Wyszomirski, Margaret J. (1987). "The Commissioning of a Work of Public Sculpture." *Public Art/Public Controversy: The Tilted Arc on Trial.* American Council for the Arts. New York: ACA Books. 18–27.

Ball, Edward. (1993). "To Theme or Not to Theme: Disneyfication Without Guilt." *The Once and Future Park.* Deborah Karasov and Steve Waryan (eds.). Princeton: Princeton Architectural Press. 31–7.

Barreneche, Raul. (2006). "Viewing Rooms." *Travel + Leisure* (June). http://www.travelandleisure.com/articles/viewing-rooms&printer=1. Accessed 7 Jan. 2007.

Beardsley, John. (1981a). *Art in Public Places.* Washington, DC: National Endowment for the Arts/Partners for Livable Places.

Beardsley, John. (1981b). "Personal Sensibilities in Public Places." *Artforum* 19.10 (June/Summer): 43–5.

Beardsley, John. (1995). *Gardens of Revelation: Environments by Visionary Artists.* New York: Abbeville Press.

Blake, Peter. (1974). *Form Follows Fiasco: Why Modern Architecture Hasn't Worked.* Boston: Little, Brown, and Company.

Blake, Peter. (1987). "Public Art." *Interior Design* (Mar.): 286–7.

Boon, James A. (1991). "Why Museums Make Me Sad." *Exhibiting Cultures: The Poetics and Politics of Museum Display.* Ivan Karp and Steven D. Lavine (eds.). Washington, DC: Smithsonian Institution Press. 255–77.

Boswell, Peter. (1991). "Sculpture Gardens." *Public Art Review* 6 (Fall/Winter). http://publicartreview.org/pdf/boswell.pdf. Accessed 26 Jan. 2007.

Bourdieu, Pierre. (1984). "The Aesthetic Sense as the Sense of Distinction." *Consumer Society Reader.* Juliet B. Schor and Douglas B. Holt (eds.). New York: New Press, 2000. 205–11.

Bibliography

Boyer, M. Christine. (1992). "Cities for Sale: Merchandising History at South Street Seaport." *Variations on a Theme Park: The New American City and the End of Public Space.* Michael Sorkin (ed.). New York: Noonday-Hill and Wang. 181–204.

Breitbart, Myrna Margulles, and Worden, Pamela. (1993). *Beyond a "Sense of Place": New Roles for the Arts and Humanities in Urban Revitalization.* Boston: UrbanArts.

Brenson, Michael. (1996). "The Sculpture Object." *Sculpture* 15.9 (Nov.): 30–3.

Broude, Norma. (1991). "Report from Washington II: Alternative Monuments." *Art in America* 79.2 (Feb.): 72–3, 75, 77, 79, 81.

Buchwalter, Andrew (ed.). (1992). *Culture and Democracy: Social and Ethical Issues in Public Support for the Arts and Humanities.* Boulder: Westview Press.

Bukatman, Scott. (1995). "The Artificial Infinite: On Special Effects and the Sublime." *Visual Display: Culture Beyond Appearances.* Lynne Cooke and Peter Wollen (eds.). Seattle: Bay Press/New York: Dia Art Foundation. 255–89.

Buren, Daniel. (1975). "Function of Architecture." *Thinking About Exhibitions.* Reesa Greenberg, Bruce W. Ferguson, and Sandy Nairne (eds.). London: Routledge, 1996. 313–19.

Burke, Edmund. (1757). *A Philosophical Inquiry into the Origin of Our Ideas of the Sublime and Beautiful.* London: Bell, 1889.

Buskirk, Martha. (1991). "Moral Rights: First Step or False Start?" *Art in America* 79.7 (July): 37, 39, 41, 43, 45.

Calthorpe, Peter. (1993). *The Next American Metropolis: Ecology, Community, and the American Dream.* New York: Princeton Architectural Press.

Carlson, Peter. (1985). "A Rusty Eyesore or a Work of Art? Sculptor Richard Serra Defends His Controversial *Tilted Arc.*" *People Weekly* 23 (1 Apr.): 138–40.

Chadwick, Whitney. (1995). "Women Who Run with the Brushes and Glue." *Confessions of the Guerrilla Girls.* Guerrilla Girls. New York: Harper Perennial. 7–11.

(2006). "Chicago's Millennium Park Becomes the Nation's First Cultural Destination to Offer Free MP3 Audio Tours for Download." http://egov.cityofchicago.org/city/weboritak/jsp/content. Accessed 22 Sept. 2006.

City of Chicago Department of Cultural Affairs. (2005). *The Chicago Public Art Guide.* Chicago: Chicago Office of Tourism.

Clark, Erin. (2006). "Can You Hear Me Now?" *Artworks* (Fall): 32–3.

Cockcroft, Eva, Weber, John, and Cockcroft, James. (1977). *Toward a People's Art: The Contemporary Mural Movement.* New York: Dutton.

Cockcroft, Eva. (1991). "L.A.'s Mural Boom: Writing on the Wall." *New Art Examiner* (Nov.): 20–4.

160

Corrin, Lisa, and Sangster, Gary. (1994). "Culture *Is* Action: Action in Chicago." *Sculpture* 13.2 (Mar.–Apr.): 30–5.

Cowley, Jennifer. (2001). "Public Art in Private Spaces: Amarillo's Unusual Signs." *Tierra Grande: Quarterly of the Real Estate Center at Texas A&M University* (Oct.).

Crawford, Margaret. (1992). "The World in a Shopping Mall." *Variations on a Theme Park: The New American City and the End of Public Space.* Michael Sorkin (ed.). New York: Noonday-Hill and Wang. 3–30.

Crew, Spencer R., and Sims, James E. (1991). "Locating Authenticity: Fragments of a Dialogue." *Exhibiting Cultures: The Poetics and Politics of Museum Display.* Ivan Karp and Steven D. Lavine (eds.). Washington, DC: Smithsonian Institution Press. 159–75.

Crichton, E. G. (1992). "Is the NAMES Quilt Art?" *Critical Issues in Public Art: Content, Context, and Controversy.* Harriet F. Senie and Sally Webster (eds.). 1998 rev. edn. Washington, DC: Smithsonian Institution Press. 287–94.

Crow, Thomas. (1996). *Modern Art in the Common Culture.* New Haven: Yale University Press.

Danto, Arthur C. (1987). *The State of the Art.* New York: Prentice Hall.

Dean, Cornelia. (2003). "Drawn to the Lightning." *New York Times* 21 Sept. http://query.nytimes.com/gstfullpage.html: query for Lightning Field. Accessed 16 Oct. 2006.

Debord, Guy. (1967). *The Society of the Spectacle.* Donald Nicolson-Smith (trans.). New York: Zone Books, 1995.

Decter, Joshua. (1997). "GALA Committee, January 16–March 7, 1998." http://www.grandarts.com/exhibits/Gala.html. Accessed 29 Jan. 2007.

Deitch, Jeffrey. (1983). "The New Economics of Environmental Art." *Art in the Land: A Critical Anthology of Environmental Art.* Alan Sonfist (ed.). New York: Dutton. 85–91.

De Montebello, Philippe. (2004). "Art Museums, Inspiring Public Trust." *Whose Muse? Art Museums and the Public Trust.* James Cuno (ed.). Princeton: Princeton University Press/Cambridge: Harvard University Art Museums. 151–69.

Dempsey, Amy. (2006). *Destination Art.* Berkeley: University of California Press.

Dery, Mark. (1999). *The Pyrotechnic Insanitarium: American Culture on the Brink.* New York: Grove Press.

Deutsche, Rosalyn. (1992). "Public Art and Its Uses." *Critical Issues in Public Art: Content, Context, and Controversy.* Harriet F. Senie and Sally Webster (eds.). 1998 rev. edn. Washington, DC: Smithsonian Institution Press. 158–70.

Deutsche, Rosalyn. (1996). *Evictions: Art and Spatial Politics.* Cambridge: MIT Press.

Dewey, John. (1927). *The Public and Its Problems*. Athens: Swallow Press, 1988.

Dimitrijevic, Nena. (1987). "Meanwhile, in the Real World." *Flash Art* 134 (May): 44–9.

Doezema, Marianne. (1977). "The Public Monument in Tradition and Transition." *The Public Monument and Its Audience*. Doezema and June Hargrove. Cleveland: Cleveland Museum of Art. 9–21.

Doss, Erika. (1992). "Raising Community Consciousness with Public Art: Contrasting Projects by Judy Baca and Andrew Leicester." *American Art* 6.1 (Winter): 62–81.

Doss, Erika. (1995). *Spirit Poles and Flying Pigs: Public Art and Cultural Democracy in American Communities*. Washington, DC: Smithsonian Institution Press.

Dubin, Steven C. (1992). *Arresting Images: Impolitic Art and Uncivil Actions*. London: Routledge.

Duchamp, Marcel. (1957). "The Creative Act." *Theories and Documents of Contemporary Art: A Sourcebook of Artists' Writings*. Kristine Stiles and Peter Selz (eds.). Berkeley: University of California Press, 1996. 818–19.

Duncan, Carol. (1991). "Art Museums and the Ritual of Citizenship." *Exhibiting Cultures: The Poetics and Politics of Museum Display*. Ivan Karp and Steven D. Lavine (eds.). Washington, DC: Smithsonian Institution Press. 88–103.

Dziewior, Yilmaz. (2000). "GALA Committee." *Artforum* (Summer). http://www.findarticles.com/p/articles/mi_m0268/is_10_38_/ai_65071360. Accessed 29 Jan. 2007.

Eastwood, Dina. (2006). "Dina Talks with Steve Wynn." *Artworks* (Fall): 60–5.

Eco, Umberto. (1975). "Travels in Hyperreality." *Travels in Hyperreality: Essays*. William Weaver (trans.). San Diego: Harcourt Brace Jovanovich, 1986. 3–58.

Edgers, Geoff. (2006). "How they did it." *Boston Globe* 6 Dec.: K4–K7.

Edson, Gary, and Dean, David. (1994). *The Handbook for Museums*. London: Routledge.

Ehrenhalt, Alan. (1994). "When the Art Critic Is the Taxpayer." *Governing* 7 (June): 9–10.

Elsen, Albert. (1989a). "Public Rights and Critics' Failures." *Art News* 88.2 (Feb.): 174.

Elsen, Albert. (1989b). "What We Have Learned about Modern Public Sculpture." *Art Journal* 48.4 (Winter): 291–7.

Falk, John H., and Dierking, Lynn D. (2000). *Learning from Museums: Visitor Experiences and the Making of Meaning*. Walnut Creek: Altamira.

Feuer, Wendy. (1989). "Public Art from A Public Sector Perspective." *Art in the Public Interest*. Arlene Raven (ed.). Ann Arbor: UMI Research Press. 139–53.

Finkelpearl, Tom. (2001). *Dialogues in Public Art*. Cambridge: MIT Press.

Fjellman, Stephen. (1992). *Vinyl Leaves: Walt Disney World and America*. Boulder: Westview Press.

Fleming, David. (2002). "Positioning the Museum for Social Inclusion." *Museums, Society, and Inequality*. Richard Sandell (ed.). London: Routledge. 213–24.

Fleming, Ronald Lee, and von Tscharner, Renata. (1981). *Place Makers: Creating Public Art That Tells You Where You Are*. Boston: Harcourt Brace Jovanovich, 1987.

Foote, Nancy. (1980). "Sightings on Siting." *Urban Encounters: Art, Architecture, Audience*. Philadelphia: Institute of Contemporary Art/University of Pennsylvania. 25–34.

Foster, Hal. (1985). *Recodings: Art, Spectacle, Cultural Politics*. Seattle: Bay Press.

Foster, Hal (ed.). (1987). *Discussions in Contemporary Culture (Number One)*. Seattle: Bay Press/New York: Dia Art Foundation.

Francaviglia, Richard. (1996). *Main Street Revisited: Time, Space and Image Building in Small-Town America*. Iowa City: University of Iowa Press.

Freedman, Susan K., et al. (2004). *Plop: Recent Projects of the Public Art Fund*. London: Merrell/New York: Public Art Fund.

Freudenheim, Susan. (1988). "Under the Singing Eucalyptus Tree." *Artforum* 26.8 (Apr.): 124–30.

Gaiter, Colette. (1995). "Private Broadcasts/Public Conversations." *Public Art Review* 13 (Fall/Winter). http://publicartreview.org/pdf/gaiter.pdf. Accessed 26 Jan. 2007.

Gamble, Allison. (1994). "Reframing a Movement: Sculpture Chicago's 'Culture in Action'." *New Art Examiner* 21.5 (Jan.): 18–23.

Gans, Herbert J. (1974). *Popular Culture and High Culture: An Analysis and Evaluation of Taste*. New York: Basic Books.

Gee, Maria. (1995). "Yes in My Front Yard: Community Participation and the Public Art Process." *High Performance* (Spring/Summer): 60–5.

Geer, Suvan, and Rowe, Sandra. (1995). "Thoughts on Graffiti as Public Art." *Public Art Review* 12 (Spring/Summer). http://publicartreview.org/pdf/geer.pdf. Accessed 26 Jan. 2007.

Ghirardo, Diane. (1996). *Architecture After Modernism*. London: Thames & Hudson.

Gibson, Todd. (2004a). "A Pilgrimage to *The Lightning Field* (Part 1 of 2); 21 July 2004." *From the Floor* website. http://fromthefloor.blogspot.com/2004/07/pilgrimage-to-lightning-field-part-1.html. Accessed 16 Oct. 2006.

Gibson, Todd. (2004b). "A Pilgrimage to *The Lightning Field* (Part 2 of 2); 25 July 2004." *From the Floor* website. http://fromthefloor.blogspot. com/2004/07/pilgrimage-to-lightning-field-part-2.html. Accessed 16 Oct. 2006.

Goldstein, Barbara (ed.). (2005). *Public Art by the Book.* Seattle: University of Washington Press/Americans for the Arts.

Grant, Daniel. (1989). "Public Art and Its Inherent Problems." *American Artist* (Oct.): 78–9, 81–4.

(2007). "Grants for Arts Projects." Official website of the National Endowment for the Arts. http://arts.endow.gov/grants/apply/Visualarts.html. Accessed 11 Jan. 2007.

Graves, Donna. (1993). "Sharing Space." *Public Art Review* 8 (Spring/Summer). http://publicartreview.org/pdf/graves.pdf. Accessed 26 Jan. 2007.

Greenblatt, Stephen. (1991). "Resonance and Wonder." *Exhibiting Cultures: The Poetics and Politics of Museum Display.* Ivan Karp and Steven D. Lavine (eds.). Washington, DC: Smithsonian Institution Press. 42–56.

Gude, Olivia. (1989). "An Aesthetics of Collaboration." *Art Journal* 48.4 (Winter): 321–3.

Gurian, Elaine Heumann. (1990). "The Concept of Fairness: A Debate at the American Association of Museums." *Civilizing the Museum: The Collected Writings of Elaine Heumann Gurian.* London: Routledge, 2006. 11–13.

Gurian, Elaine Heumann. (1991). "Noodling Around with Exhibition Opportunities." *Exhibiting Cultures: The Poetics and Politics of Museum Display.* Ivan Karp and Steven D. Lavine (eds.). Washington, DC: Smithsonian Institution Press. 176–90.

Gurian, Elaine Heumann. (2001). "Function Follows Form: How Mixed-Use Spaces in Museums Build Community." *Civilizing the Museum: The Collected Writings of Elaine Heumann Gurian.* London: Routledge, 2006. 99–114.

Habermas, Jürgen. (1962). *The Structural Transformation of the Public Sphere: An Inquiry Into a Category of Bourgeois Society.* Thomas Burger and Frederick Lawrence (trans.). Cambridge: MIT Press, 1989.

Halbreich, Kathy. (1984). "The Social Dimension: Art That's More 'As' Than 'On'." *Insights/On Sights: Perspectives on Art in Public Places.* Stacy Paleologos Harris (ed.). Washington, DC: Partners for Livable Places. 48–60.

Hall, Carol. (1983). "Environmental Artists: Sources and Directions." *Art in the Land: A Critical Anthology of Environmental Art.* Alan Sonfist (ed.). New York: Dutton. 8–59.

Hannigan, John. (1998). *Fantasy City: Pleasure and Profit in the Postmodern Metropolis.* New York: Routledge.

Harries, Mags, and Héder, Lajos. (2006). Author's interview with artists, 21 Aug.

Harris, Jonathan. (1995). *Federal Art and National Culture: The Politics of Identity in New Deal America.* Cambridge: Cambridge University Press.

Harvey, David. (1980). *The Condition of Postmodernity: An Enquiry into the Origins of Cultural Change.* Oxford: Basil Blackwell, 1990.

Hawkins, Peter S. (1993). "Naming Names: The Art of Memory and the NAMES Project AIDS Quilt." *Critical Inquiry* 19.4 (Summer): 752–79.

Hayden, Dolores. (1992). "An American Sense of Place." *Critical Issues in Public Art: Content, Context, and Controversy.* Harriet F. Senie and Sally Webster (eds.). 1998 rev. edn. Washington, DC: Smithsonian Institution Press. 261–9.

Hayden, Dolores. (1995). *The Power of Place: Urban Landscapes as Public History.* Cambridge: MIT Press.

Hayden, Dolores. (2006). "A Field Guide to Sprawl: How to Read Everyday American Landscapes." Talk presented at Radcliffe Institute for Advanced Study, Harvard University, 20 Nov.

Heartney, Eleanor. (1993). "The Dematerialization of Public Art." *Sculpture* 12.2 (Mar.–Apr.): 44–9.

Heartney, Eleanor, Gopnik, Adam, et al. (2005). *City Art: New York's Percent for Art Program.* London: Merrell/New York: New York City Department of Cultural Affairs.

Hein, Hilde. (1996). "What is Public Art? Time, Place and Meaning." *Journal of Aesthetics and Art Criticism* 54.1 (Winter): 1–7.

Hein, Hilde S. (2000). *The Museum in Transition: A Philosophical Perspective.* Washington, DC: Smithsonian Institution Press.

Hein, Hilde. (2006). *Public Art: Thinking Museums Differently.* Lanham: AltaMira.

Hine, Thomas. (2001). "The Art of Identity." *New-Land-Marks: Public Art, Community, and the Meaning of Place.* Penny Balkin Bach (ed.). Washington, DC: Editions Ariel/Philadelphia: Fairmount Park Art Association. 36–44.

Hixson, Kathryn. (1998). "Icons and Interventions in Chicago: And the Potential of Public Art." *Sculpture* 17.5 (May–June): 46–51.

Hochfield, Sylvia. (1988). "The Moral Rights (and Wrongs) of Public Art." *Art News* 87.5 (May): 143–6.

Holmstrom, David. (1996). "Boston's 'Big Dig' Hits a Ditch in Funds." *Christian Science Monitor* 88.103 (Apr. 23). Academic Search Premier, EBSCO, Emerson College Library. Accessed 5 Nov. 2004.

Hooper-Greenhill, Eilean. (1994). *Museums and Their Visitors.* London: Routledge.

Horkheimer, Max, and Adorno, Theodor W. (1944). "The Culture Industry: Enlightenment as Mass Deception." *Dialectic of Enlightenment.* John Cumming (trans.). London: Lane, 1973. 120–67.

Howarth, Kathryn. (1985). "'Tilted Arc' Hearing." *Art News* 23.10 (Summer): 98–9.

Hughes, Robert. (1985). "The Trials of *Tilted Arc.*" *Time* (3 June): 78.

Hunter, Sam. (1985). "The Public Agency as Patron." *Art for the Public: The Collection of the Port Authority of New York and New Jersey.* New York: Port Authority of New York and New Jersey.

Huxtable, Ada Louise. (1997). *The Unreal America: Architecture and Illusion.* New York: New Press.

Institute for Infinitely Small Things. (2006). "The Institute Speaks." Talk presented at Carpenter Center for the Visual Arts, Harvard University, 27 Nov.

Jacob, Mary Jane. (1995). "Outside the Loop." *Culture in Action.* Jacob, Michael Brenson, and Eva M. Olson. Seattle: Bay Press. 50–61.

Jacobs, Jane. (1961). *The Death and Life of Great American Cities.* New York: Vintage Books-Random House, 1992.

Jameson, Fredric. (1991). *Postmodernism, or, the Cultural Logic of Late Capitalism.* Durham: Duke University Press.

Jenkins, Henry, McPherson, Tara, and Shattuc, Jane. (2002). "Defining Popular Culture." *Hop on Pop: The Politics and Pleasures of Popular Culture.* Jenkins, McPherson, and Shattuc (eds.). Durham: Duke University Press. 26–42.

Johnson, David. (1994). "Las Vegas: Buccaneer Bay." *Theatre Crafts International* (May): 34–7.

Johnson, Ken. (1990). "Poetry and Public Service." *Art in America* 151 (Mar.): 160–3, 219.

Jordanova, Ludmilla. (1989). "Objects of Knowledge: A Historical Perspective on Museums." *The New Museology.* Peter Vergo (ed.). London: Reaktion Books. 22–40.

Joselit, David. (1989). "Lessons in Public Sculpture." *Art in America* (Dec.): 130–5.

Joselit, David. (1990). "Public Art and the Public Purse." *Art in America* (July): 142–51, 183.

Kangas, Matthew. (1980). "Earthworks: Land Reclamation as Sculpture." *Vanguard* 9.1 (Feb.): 16–21.

Kaprow, Allan, and Smithson, Robert. (1967). "What is a Museum? A Dialogue between Allan Kaprow and Robert Smithson." *Arts Yearbook.* Reprinted in *The Writings of Robert Smithson.* Nancy Holt (ed.). New York: New York University Press, 1979. 59–66.

Kardon, Janet. (1980). "Street Wise/Street Foolish." *Urban Encounters: Art, Architecture, Audience.* Philadelphia: Institute of Contemporary Art/ University of Pennsylvania. 8–14.

Karp, Ivan, and Wilson, Fred. (1993). "Constructing the Spectacle of Culture in Museums." *Thinking About Exhibitions.* Reesa Greenberg, Bruce W. Ferguson, and Sandy Nairne (eds.). London: Routledge, 1996. 251–67.

Kastner, Jeffrey. (2005). "Social Fabric." *Artforum International* 43.9 (May): 65(2). Academic Search Premier, EBSCO, Emerson College Library. Accessed 15 Aug. 2006.

Katz, Stanley N. (1984). "Influences on Public Policies in the United States." *The Arts and Public Policy in the United States*. American Assembly. Englewood Cliffs: Prentice-Hall. 23–37.

Kayden, Jerold S., et al. (2000). *Privately Owned Public Space: The New York City Experience*. New York: Wiley.

Kaye, Nick E. (2000). *Site-Specific Art: Performance, Place and Documentation*. London: Routledge.

Kelly, Michael. (1996). "Public Art Controversies: The Serra and Lin Cases." *Journal of Aesthetics and Art Criticism*. 54.1 (Winter): 15–22.

Kirshenblatt-Gimblett, Barbara. (1998). *Destination Culture: Tourism, Museums, and Heritage*. Berkeley: University of California Press.

Knight, Cheryl Krause. (2000). *The Mouse that Walt Built: Contemporary Contextual Readings of Disney World*. Dissertation. Philadelphia: Temple University. UMI Dissertation Services.

Knight, Cher Krause. (2002). "Beyond the Neon Billboard: Sidewalk Spectacle and Public Art in Las Vegas." *Journal of American and Comparative Cultures* 25.1–2 (Spring/Summer): 9–13.

Kotler, Neil, and Kotler, Philip. (1998). *Museum Strategy and Marketing: Designing Missions, Building Audiences, Generating Revenue and Resources*. San Francisco: Jossey-Bass.

Kramer, Jane. (1994). *Whose Art Is It?* Durham: Duke University Press.

Kunstler, James Howard. (1993). *The Geography of Nowhere: The Rise and Decline of America's Man-Made Landscape*. New York: Simon & Schuster.

Kwon, Miwon. (2002). *One Place After Another: Site-Specific Art and Locational Identity*. Cambridge: MIT Press, 2004.

Lacy, Suzanne. (1995). *Mapping the Terrain: New Genre Public Art*. Seattle: Bay Press.

Le Corbusier (Charles-Edouard Jeanneret). (1929). "A Contemporary City." *The City Reader*. Richard Legates and Frederic Stout (eds.). 3rd edn. New York: Routledge, 1996. 317–24.

Lefebvre, Henri. (1996). *Writings on Cities*. Eleanore Kofman and Elizabeth Lebas (trans.). Oxford: Blackwell.

Levine, Lawrence W. (1988). *Highbrow/Lowbrow: The Emergence of Cultural Hierarchy in America*. Cambridge: Harvard University Press.

Levitt, Arthur, Jr. (1991). "Introduction." *Public Money and the Museum: Essays on Government Funding for the Arts*. Stephen Benedict (ed.). New York: Norton. 19–30.

Lewis, JoAnn. (1977). "A Modern Medici for Public Art." *Art News* 76.4 (Apr.): 36–40.

(2006). "Lightning Field." Dia Art Foundation official website. http://www. lightningfield.org. Accessed 19 Sept. 2006.

Lin, Maya. (2005). "Maya Lin in Conversation with Louis Menand." Talk presented at Carpenter Center for the Visual Arts, Harvard University, 1 Dec.

Lippard, Lucy. (1967/68). "Beauty and the Bureaucracy." *Hudson Review* 20.4 (Winter). Reprinted in *Changing*. New York: Dutton, 1971. 227–36.

Lippard, Lucy. (1969/70). "Prefatory Notes." *Changing*. New York: Dutton, 1971. 11–13.

Lippard, Lucy R. (1977a). "This is Art? The Alienation of the Avant Garde from the Audience." *Seven Days* (14 Feb.). Reprinted in *Get the Message?: A Decade of Art for Social Change*. New York: Dutton, 1984. 73–9.

Lippard, Lucy R. (1977b). "Community and Outreach: Art Outdoors, in the Public Domain (Excerpts from a Slide Lecture)." *Studio International* (Mar.–Apr.). Reprinted in *Get the Message?: A Decade of Art for Social Change*. New York: Dutton, 1984. 36–44.

Lippard, Lucy R. (1989). "Moving Targets/Moving Out." *Art in the Public Interest*. Arlene Raven (ed.). New York: Da Capo Press, 1993. 209–28.

Lippard, Lucy R. (1990). *Mixed Blessings: New Art in a Multicultural America*. New York: Pantheon Books.

Lippard, Lucy R. (1999). *On the Beaten Track: Tourism, Art and Place*. New York: New Press.

Lofland, Lyn H. (1998). *The Public Realm: Exploring the City's Quintessential Social Territory*. New York: Aldine de Gruyter.

Lurie, David V., and Wodiczko, Krzysztof. (1988). "Homeless Vehicle Project." *October* 47 (Winter): 53–67.

MacCannell, Dean. (1973). "Staged Authenticity: Arrangements of Social Space in Tourist Settings." *American Journal of Sociology* 79: 589–603.

Mainardi, Patricia. (1973). "Quilts: The Great American Art." *Feminist Art Journal* 2.1 (Winter). Reprinted in *Feminism and Art History: Questioning the Litany*. Norma Broude and Mary D. Garrard (eds.). New York: Harper-Row, 1982. 331–46.

Mainardi, Patricia. (1988). "Quilt Survivals and Revivals." *Arts Magazine* 62.9 (May): 49–53.

Maksymowicz, Virginia. (1990). "Through the Back Door: Alternative Approaches to Public Art." *Art and the Public Sphere*. W. J. T. Mitchell (ed.). Chicago: University of Chicago Press, 1990. 147–57.

Mankin, Lawrence. (1982). "Government Patronage: An Historical Overview." *Public Policy and the Arts*. Kevin V. Mulcahy and C. Richard Swaim (eds.). Boulder: Westview Press. 111–40.

Marling, Karal Ann. (1984). *The Colossus of Roads: Myth and Symbol along the American Highway*. Minneapolis: University of Minnesota Press.

Marter, Joan. (1989). "Collaborations: Artists and Architects on Public Sites." *Art Journal* 48.4 (Winter): 315–20.

Matzner, Florian (ed.). (2001). *Public Art*. Munich: Hatje Cantz Verlag.

McClellan, Andrew (ed.). (2003). *Art and Its Publics: Museum Studies at the Millennium*. Malden: Blackwell.

McConathy, Dale. (1987). "Serra's Unofficial Monument." *Public Art/Public Controversy: The Tilted Arc on Trial*. American Council for the Arts. New York: ACA Books. 3–17.

McKee, Alan. (2005). *The Public Sphere: An Introduction*. Cambridge: Cambridge University Press.

McKinley, Jesse. (2007). "A Changing Battle on AIDS is Reflected in a Quilt." *New York Times* 31 Jan. http://www.nytimes.com/2007/01/31/us/31quilt.html. Accessed 31 Jan. 2007.

McKinzie, Richard D. (1973). *The New Deal for Artists*. Princeton: Princeton University Press.

McNichol, Dan. (2001). *The Big Dig at Night*. New York: Silver Lining Books.

McNichol, Dan. (2002a). *The Big Dig*. New York: Silver Lining Books.

McNichol, Dan. (2002b). *The Big Dig Trivia Quiz Book*. New York: Silver Lining Books.

Medvedow, Jill. (2004). "Contours and Context: Five Years of Vita Brevis." *Vita Brevis: History, Landscape, and Art 1998–2003*. Jill Medvedow and Carole Anne Meehan. Boston: Institute of Contemporary Art/Göttingen: Steidl. 9–16.

Miles, Malcolm. (1989). *Art for Public Places: Critical Essays*. Winchester: Winchester School of Arts Press.

Miles, Malcolm. (1997). *Art, Space and the City: Public Art and Urban Futures*. London/New York: Routledge.

Miles, Malcolm. (2004). *Urban Avant-Gardes: Art, Architecture and Change*. London: Routledge.

(2006). "Millennium Park." Official website. http://www.millenniumpark.org. Accessed 22 Sept. 2006.

Mitchell, W. J. T. (ed.). (1990). *Art and the Public Sphere*. Chicago: University of Chicago Press.

Morgan, Jessica. (2004). "Introduction." *Vita Brevis: History, Landscape, and Art 1998–2003*. Jill Medvedow and Carole Anne Meehan. Boston: Institute of Contemporary Art/Göttingen: Steidl. 7.

Morris, Robert. (1992). "Earthworks: Land Reclamation as Sculpture." *Critical Issues in Public Art: Content, Context, and Controversy*. Harriet F. Senie and Sally Webster (eds.). 1998 rev. edn. Washington, DC: Smithsonian Institution Press. 250–60.

Mumford, Lewis. (1938). *The Culture of Cities*. New York: Harcourt Brace Jovanovich, 1970.

169

Netzer, Dick. (1978). *The Subsidized Muse: Public Support for the Arts in the United States.* Cambridge: Cambridge University Press.

Newman, Morris. (1995). "The Strip Meets the Flaming Volcano." *Progressive Architecture* (Feb.): 82–6.

Novelli, Lynn R. (1996). "Public Commissions: Budgeting for Real Costs." *Sculpture* 15.1 (Jan.): 32–5.

O'Doherty, Brian. (1974). "Public Art and the Government: A Progress Report." *Art in America* 62.3 (May–June): 44–9.

O'Doherty, Brian. (1976). *The White Cube: The Ideology of the Gallery Space.* Santa Monica: Lapis Press, 1986.

O'Doherty, Brian. (1981). "The Gallery as a Gesture." *Thinking About Exhibitions.* Reesa Greenberg, Bruce W. Ferguson, and Sandy Nairne (eds.). London: Routledge, 1996. 321–40.

Owens, Craig. (1987). "The Birth and Death of the Viewer: The Yen for Art." *Discussions in Contemporary Culture (Number One).* Hal Foster (ed.). Seattle: Bay Press/New York: Dia Art Foundation. 16–23.

Park, Marlene, and Markowitz, Gerald E. (1984). *Democratic Vistas: Post Offices and Public Art in the New Deal.* Philadelphia: Temple University Press.

Park, Marlene, and Markowitz, Gerald E. (1992). "New Deal for Public Art." *Critical Issues in Public Art: Content, Context, and Controversy.* Harriet F. Senie and Sally Webster (eds.). 1998 rev. edn. Washington, DC: Smithsonian Institution Press. 128–41.

Perreault, John. (1978). "False Objects: Duplicates, Replicas and Types." *Artforum* 16.6 (Feb.): 24–7.

Phillips, Patricia C. (1988). "Out of Order: The Public Art Machine." *Artforum* 27.4 (Dec.): 92–7.

Phillips, Patricia C. (1992). "Temporality and Public Art." *Critical Issues in Public Art: Content, Context, and Controversy.* Harriet F. Senie and Sally Webster (eds.). 1998 rev. edn. Washington, DC: Smithsonian Institution Press. 295–304.

Phillips, Patricia C. (1999). "Dynamic Exchange: Public Art at This Time." *Public Art Review* 21 (Fall/Winter). http://publicartreview.org/pdf/phillips2.pdf. Accessed 26 Jan. 2007.

Plagens, Peter. (1989). "The McSacred and the Profane." *Art Criticism* 5.1: 19–33.

Powers, Lynn A. (1996). "Whatever Happened to the Graffiti Art Movement?" *Journal of Popular Culture* 29.4 (Spring): 137–42.

Princenthal, Nancy. (1984). "Art with Designs on the Public Domain." *Industrial Design* 31 (Mar.–Apr.): 44–9.

Princenthal, Nancy. (1987). "Social Seating." *Art in America* 75.6 (June): 130–7.

Prokopoff, Stephen. (1981). "The Government as Patron." *Collaboration: Artists and Architects.* Barbaralee Diamonstein (ed.). New York: Whitney Library of Design/Watson-Guptill. 78–87.

Ramljak, Suzanne. (1992). "Interview: Mary Jane Jacob." *Sculpture* (May–June): 20–2.

Ratcliff, Carter. (1988). "The Marriage of Art and Money." *Theories of Contemporary Art.* Richard Hertz (ed.). 2nd edn. Upper Saddle River: Prentice Hall, 1993. 269–82.

Rathbone, Perry T. (1984). "Influences of Private Patrons: The Art Museum as an Example." *The Arts and Public Policy in the United States.* American Assembly. Englewood Cliffs: Prentice-Hall. 38–56.

Raven, Arlene (ed.). (1989). *Art in the Public Interest.* New York: Da Capo Press, 1993.

Rectanus, Mark W. (2002). *Culture Incorporated: Museums, Artists, and Corporate Sponsorships.* Minneapolis: University of Minnesota Press.

Redstone, Louis G. (with Ruth R. Redstone). (1981). *Public Art: New Directions.* New York: McGraw-Hill.

Rice, Danielle. (1992). "The 'Rocky' Dilemma: Museums, Monuments, and Popular Culture in the Postmodern Era." *Critical Issues in Public Art: Content, Context, and Controversy.* Harriet F. Senie and Sally Webster (eds.). 1998 rev. edn. Washington, DC: Smithsonian Institution Press. 228–36.

Richardson, Brenda (with the assistance of Trish Waters). (1986). *Scott Burton.* Baltimore: Baltimore Museum of Art.

Ritzer, George. (1998). *The McDonaldization Thesis: Explorations and Extensions.* London: Sage.

Robinson, Charles Mulford. (1903). *Modern Civic Art or, The City Made Beautiful.* New York: Arno Press, 1970. Reprint of 4th rev. edn. of 1918.

Rosen, Miriam. (1996). "Web-Specific Works: The Internet as a Space for Public Art." *Art & Design* 11.1–2 (Jan.–Feb.): 87–95.

Rosenthal, Mark. (1983). "Some Attitudes of Earth Art: From Competition to Adoration." *Art in the Land: A Critical Anthology of Environmental Art.* Alan Sonfist (ed.). New York: Dutton, 1983. 60–72.

Rosler, Martha. (1987). "The Birth and Death of the Viewer: On the Public Function of Art." *Discussions in Contemporary Culture (Number One).* Hal Foster (ed.). Seattle: Bay Press/New York: Dia Art Foundation. 9–15.

Rosler, Martha. (1991). "Fragments of a Metropolitan Viewpoint." *If You Lived Here: The City in Art, Theory, and Social Activism.* Martha Rosler. Brian Wallis (ed.). Seattle: Bay Press. 15–43.

Ross, Andrew. (1989). *No Respect: Intellectuals and Popular Culture.* New York: Routledge.

Rosser, Phyllis. (1989). "Education Through Collaboration Saves Lives." *Art in the Public Interest.* Arlene Raven (ed.). Ann Arbor: UMI Research Press. 127–38.

Sabal, Robert. (2006). Author's interview with member of the Institute for Infinitely Small Things, 28 June.

Saunders, William S. (ed.). (2005). *Commodification and Spectacle in Architecture (A Harvard Design Magazine Reader)*. Minneapolis: University of Minnesota Press.

Schama, Simon. (1995). *Landscape and Memory*. New York: Vintage-Random House.

Schneider, William. (2000). "The Big Dig and the Shovel Brigade." *National Journal* 32.17 (Apr. 22). Academic Search Premier, EBSCO, Emerson College Library. Accessed 5 Nov. 2004.

Schwartz, Andrew (ed.). (2000). *Public Parks, Private Partners: How Partnerships are Revitalizing Urban Parks*. New York: Project for Public Spaces, Inc.

Senie, Harriet. (1984). "The Right Stuff." *Art News* 83.3 (Mar.): 50–9.

Senie, Harriet F. (1989). "Richard Serra's '*Tilted Arc*': Art and Non-Art Issues." *Art Journal* 48.4 (Winter): 298–302.

Senie, Harriet F. (1992a). "Baboons, Pet Rocks, and Bomb Threats: Public Art and Public Perception." *Critical Issues in Public Art: Content, Context, and Controversy*. Harriet F. Senie and Sally Webster (eds.). 1998 rev. edn. Washington, DC: Smithsonian Institution Press. 237–46.

Senie, Harriet F. (1992b). *Contemporary Public Sculpture: Tradition, Transformation, and Controversy*. New York: Oxford University Press.

Senie, Harriet F. (2002). *The Tilted Arc Controversy: Dangerous Precedent?* Minneapolis: University of Minnesota Press.

Senie, Harriet F. (2003). "Reframing Public Art: Audience Use, Interpretation, and Appreciation." *Art and Its Publics: Museum Studies at the Millennium*. Andrew McClellan (ed.). Malden: Blackwell. 185–200.

Serra, Richard. (1989). "Issues and Commentary: 'Tilted Arc' Destroyed." *Art in America* (May): 34–7, 39, 41, 43, 45, 47.

Smagula, Howard J. (1983). *Currents: Contemporary Directions in the Visual Arts*. Englewood: Prentice-Hall.

Smith, Charles Saumarez. (1989). "Museums, Artefacts, and Meanings." *The New Museology*. Peter Vergo (ed.). London: Reaktion Books. 6–21.

Smith, Roberta. (1978). "Scott Burton: Designs on Minimalism." *Art in America* 66 (Nov.–Dec.): 138–40.

Smithson, Robert. (1967). "A Tour of the Monuments of Passaic, New Jersey." *Artforum* (Dec.). Reprinted in *The Writings of Robert Smithson*. Nancy Holt (ed.). New York: New York University Press, 1979. 52–7.

Smithson, Robert. (1968). "A Sedimentation of the Mind: Earth Projects." *Artforum* (Sept.). Reprinted in *The Writings of Robert Smithson*. Nancy Holt (ed.). New York: New York University Press, 1979. 117–28.

Smithson, Robert. (1973). "Frederic Law Olmsted and the Dialectical Landscape." *Artforum* (Feb.). Reprinted in *The Writings of Robert Smithson*. Nancy Holt (ed.). New York: New York University Press, 1979. 82–91.

Snodgrass, Susan. (1992). "'all here come together to mix and contend' (A Tour Through the Harold Washington Library Collection)." *New Art Examiner* 19.8 (Apr.): 18–23.

Soja, Edward W. (1989). *Postmodern Geographies: The Reassertion of Space in Critical Social Theory.* London: Verso.

Sorkin, Michael. (1992). "See You in Disneyland." *Variations on a Theme Park: The New American City and the End of Public Space.* Sorkin (ed.). New York: Noonday-Hill and Wang. 205–232.

Sorkin, Michael (ed.). (1992). *Variations on a Theme Park: The New American City and the End of Public Space.* New York: Noonday-Hill and Wang.

Spicer, Joaneath. (1994). "The Exhibition: Lecture or Conversation?" *Curator* 37 (Sept.): 185–97.

Stephens, Suzanne. (1986). "An Equitable Relationship?" *Art in America* 74 (May): 116–23.

Stern, Seth. (2003). "$14.6 Billion Later, Boston's Big Dig Wraps Up." *Christian Science Monitor* 96.18 (19 Dec.). Academic Search Premier, EBSCO, Emerson College Library. Accessed 5 Nov. 2004.

Steyn, Juliet. (1989). "Public and Private." *Art for Public Places: Critical Essays.* Malcolm Miles (ed.). Winchester: Winchester School of Arts Press. 51–8.

Storr, Robert. (1989). "*Tilted Arc*: Enemy of the People?" *Art in the Public Interest.* Arlene Raven (ed.). New York: Da Capo Press, 1993. 269–85.

Strauss, Robert. (2006). "'Rocky' Statue Makes Comeback at Museum." *New York Times* 19 Nov. http://travel.nytimes.com/2006/11/19/us/19rocky.html. Accessed 12 Feb. 2007.

Thalacker, Donald W. (1980). *The Place of Art in the World of Architecture.* New York: Chelsea House/R.R. Bowker.

Thompson, Nato, and Sholette, Gregory (eds.). (2004). *The Interventionists: Users' Manual for the Creative Disruption of Everyday Life.* Cambridge: MIT Press.

Tsipis, Yanni. (2000). *Images of America: Boston's Central Artery.* Charlestown: Arcadia.

United States General Services Administration. (1999). *WPA Artwork in Non-Federal Repositories (Ed. II).* Washington, DC: General Services Administration.

van der Marck, Jan. (1992). "Blue/Yellow Diptych." *Art in America* 80.3 (Mar.): 100–5.

Venturi, Robert, Scott Brown, Denise, and Izenour, Stephen. (1972). *Learning from Las Vegas: The Forgotten Symbolism of Architectural Form.* Cambridge: MIT Press, 1991.

Visionary Architects: Boullee, Ledoux, Lequeu. (1968). Houston: University of St. Thomas.

(2007). "Visual Arts." Official website of the National Endowment for the Arts. http://arts.endow.gov/grants/apply/Visualarts.html. Accessed 11 Jan. 2007.

Vogel, Susan. (1991). "Always True to the Object, in Our Fashion." *Exhibiting Cultures: The Poetics and Politics of Museum Display*. Ivan Karp and Steven D. Lavine (eds.). Washington, DC: Smithsonian Institution Press. 191–204.

von Ziegesar, Peter. (1995). "Report from Kansas City: Art in the Heartland." *Art in America* 83 (June): 51–5.

Wagenknecht-Harte, Kay. (1989). *Site + Sculpture: The Collaborative Design Process*. New York: Van Nostrand Reinhold.

Wallace, Michael. (1989). "Mickey Mouse History: Portraying the Past at Disney World." *History Museums in the United States: A Critical Assessment*. Warren Leon and Roy Rosenzweig (eds.). Urbana: University of Illinois Press, 1989. 158–80.

Ward, Martha. (1996). "What's Important About the History of Modern Art Exhibitions?" *Thinking About Exhibitions*. Reesa Greenberg, Bruce W. Ferguson, and Sandy Nairne (eds.). London: Routledge. 451–64.

(2005). "Wednesday, June 08, 2005: Special Feature." Rocket Boom website. http://rocketboom.com/vlog/archives/2005/06/rb_05_jun08.html. Accessed 5 Feb. 2007.

Weil, Stephen E. (1990). *Rethinking the Museum: And Other Meditations*. Washington, DC: Smithsonian Institution Press.

Weinstein, Jeff. (1989). "Names Carried into the Future: An AIDS Quilt Unfolds." *Art in the Public Interest*. Arlene Raven (ed.). New York: Da Capo Press, 1993. 43–53.

Wetenhall, John. (1993). "A Brief History of Percent-for-Art in America." *Public Art Review* 9 (Fall/Winter). http://publicartreview.org/pdf/wetenhall.pdf. Accessed 26 Jan. 2007.

Weyergraf-Serra, Clara, and Buskirk, Martha (eds.). (1991). *The Destruction of Tilted Arc: Documents*. Cambridge: MIT Press.

White, Ean. (2005). "Interstices." http://www.incendiaryarts.com/interstices/background.html. Accessed 9 Feb. 2005.

Wiley, Dan. (1991). "Unequal Development: The Two Waterfronts." *If You Lived Here: The City in Art, Theory, and Social Activism*. Martha Rosler. Brian Wallis (ed.). Seattle: Bay Press. 270–7.

Wodiczko, Krzysztof. (1987). "Strategies of Public Address: Which Media, Which Publics?" *Discussions in Contemporary Culture (Number One)*. Hal Foster (ed.). Seattle: Bay Press/New York: Dia Art Foundation. 41–5.

Wood, James N. (2004). "The Authorities of the American Art Museum." *Whose Muse? Art Museums and the Public Trust*. James Cuno (ed.). Princeton: Princeton University Press/Cambridge: Harvard University Art Museums. 103–28.

Wortz, Melinda. (1980). "Walter de Maria's *'The Lightning Field'*." *Arts Magazine* 54 (May): 170–3.

Wyszomirski, Margaret J. (1982). "Controversies in Arts Policymaking." *Public Policy and the Arts.* Kevin V. Mulcahy and C. Richard Swaim (eds.). Boulder: Westview Press. 11–31.

Young, James E. (1992). "Holocaust Memorials in America: Public Art as Process." *Critical Issues in Public Art: Content, Context, and Controversy.* Harriet F. Senie and Sally Webster (eds.). 1998 rev. edn. Washington, DC: Smithsonian Institution Press. 57–70.

Young, James E. (1993). *The Texture of Memory: Holocaust Memorials and Meaning.* New Haven: Yale University Press.

Yudice, George. (1999). "The Privatization of Culture." *Social Text* 59, 17.2 (Summer): 17–34.

Zukin, Sharon. (1995). *The Cultures of Cities.* Malden: Blackwell.

Index